"The thing about football - the important thing about football - is that it is not just about football."

Terry Pratchet

"Soccer is an art more central to our culture than anything the Arts Council deigns to recognise"

Germain Greer

Don't Let the Football Get in the Way of a Great Day Out

The passion, pleasure and pain in being a football fan

Richard Walters

Prologue and Acknowledgments

This book is a celebration of the passion of being a football fan. It doesn't matter who you support, we all share that love of football and particularly the team we support. The late Bill Shankly, the famous Liverpool FC manger once said, "Some people think football is a matter of life and death. I assure you, it's more serious than that!" For some people, he may have had a point.

I like to think the team I support is irrelevant (sales just rose to one in Portsmouth) and it's the love of your team and football generally that matters. In this book I have shared stories from 55 years of football loving, but also included some stories from friends who are fans of clubs around the country, who have been kind enough to open up to me and tell me of their own football emotions, some painful, some inspiring and some a bit worrying.

Thank you, Jon, Alan, Stuart, John, Paul and Tristan and apologies that I have no lady contributors. It's not that women don't love football or that I'm a male chauvinist who has no female friends. The reality is that now around 26% of people attending Premier League games are female, but in the 1970s or 1980s the figures aren't even available, as I assume, they weren't deemed important enough to even measure, but my guess is less than 10%. How we have moved for the better!

I did think of renaming Jon to Jane or 'Paul the Greek' to 'Paula the Greek', to be more politically correct, but that seemed crazy and essentially, letting the tail wag the dog. That's my excuse and I think it's reasonable – but apologies anyway ladies!

I'm sure when you read of these stories, you will warmly (or maybe through clenched teeth) relive your own memories and experiences I hope so.

Thank you to my wife Marion for putting up with my love of football, even though she hates football herself. Honestly, hard to believe, but it's true!

Thank you to Glenn Jones for his creative input in designing the covers for all my books and helping me through the publication process. The last thank you must go to my dear, much loved and much missed dad, who hooked me, showed me how to love my team and football, but also how to lose gracefully when it was necessary and always to keep it in perspective. Given the club he introduced me to, it was important I learned to lose with grace and acceptance. Perhaps this was his form football Jonnie Cash's, "A Boy Named Sue" (look it up and all will be clear)!

How Dad and I cried on 1st May 1976, at our team's one and only greatest day (they won the FA Cup) and he would have hated the 25th October 2019 when my team lost 9-0 at home to Leicester City, but still took it on the chin. Such are the extreme highs and lows of being a fan!

Doesn't being a football fan, as I'm sure you are too, involve times of pain (whoever you support), a lifetime of passion and sometimes even pleasure? Let's take a look together at where this pain, passion and pleasure comes from.

Oh, and one last thing, thank you for reading my book and our stories, I hope you enjoy it.

Chapters

1 No Going Back After That!

2 They Were Tin Shacks, But We Loved Them!

3 The Magic of the FA Cup

4 Those Bitter Rivalries

5 Some People Think It's Kenneth Wolstenholme

6 Mexico 1970 and THAT Stomach Bug!

7 All Those Years and Still Hurting

8 The Blood and Thunder of the 1970s

9 Old School Hooliganism

10 Programmes and Stickers

11 Those Rare Geniuses and Classic Entertainers

12 Is Your Club a Big Club?

13 Those Gut Wrenching Moments

14 Away Day Jaunts

15 The Prawn Sandwich Affect

16 Memorably Great Teams

17 Money, Money, Money in a Rich Man's World

18 The Media – Love or Hate Them?

19 Keyboard Developments

20 European Sorties

21 Don't Let the Football Get in the Way

Chapter 1

No Going Back After That!

Mine was 27th April 1964, what was your date?

Of course, I mean your first ever football game and it's such a life changing experience, isn't it? My first game was a cold April mid-week game in 1964 and was the last game of the season and the day my dad took me to my first professional football game. I was 9 years old and I'm sure like most of us football fans, from that day forward there was no going back. I can remember the whole exciting experience like it was yesterday, which it most definitely was not. I suspect that you are remembering your own magical first match right now.

The game I was taken to was at home to Rotherham United in the old Second Division and given it was a 50:50 chance, my team ended up being Southampton, not Rotherham United. From that April evening onwards, I was a fan.

Once you have your team, you are smitten, aren't you and it just can't be changed? Some people change their wives or husbands, but your football team – no, it's not possible! When it comes to the Wives v Team game, I'm personally scoring 2-1. That says it all, although I'm so happy with both of my teams, I'm going five at the back and bringing on an extra midfielder for a forward, to hang onto what I have got. You see, in the Wives v Your Team game, away goals count double!

This book isn't about supporting my team, it's about supporting 'your team' and celebrating in the passion, pain and all too infrequent pleasure!

11

I have shared some experiences of friends who are fans of clubs around the country, to add to my own, but please don't get hung-up on the teams themselves, as this book is about the passion and the football experiences, rather than the club they support. Strangely, despite the bitter rivalries (see Chapter 4) we all have much in common and that's what we have celebrated in this book.

That fateful day for me of 27th April 1964 was a Monday and I'm not sure how my dad got my mum to agree to my attendance at an evening game, on a school day. The internet is a wonderful research facility, but even it doesn't hold details of school closures at Whitchurch Primary School in 1964. I remember the day being cold and frosty and my mum would have given my dad strict orders to, "Wrap him up." If I know my Mum, she would also have ordered him to, "Keep an eye on the boy" (me, her little 9-year-old boy), but more on this later.

We drove down in my dad's friend's car and in those days, it didn't take 25 minutes from North Hampshire to the old Dell, as it does today, more like one and a half hours on a good trip. Dad always parked some way from the ground and as we walked down the road past the old Hampshire County Cricket ground, amongst crowds of people and as a 9-year-old, I was transfixed. For a little boy, it was a magical and spine-tingling experience and I picked up on my dad and his friend's genuine excitement about going to see THEIR team.

I remember we entered through the turnstiles and at 9 years old, I could just about get my head above those ancient metal turnstiles. The walk along the corridor at the back of the stand was dark, noisy and claustrophobic and for a little boy, quite frightening. When they reached their designated mid-pitch spot, there was quite a crowd in.

Then, my dad ignored all my mum's instructions (that was nothing new) and I was passed down shoulder high by all the big strong men, until I was stood up against the touchline wall. The whole wall was filled with youngsters just like me, who also enjoyed the same shoulder high journey to the front. This probably happened in many grounds then, up and down the country at every match.

I never did tell my mum about this, as she would have berated my dad, whatever age I revealed this misdemeanour. The wall was below pitch height and you were right by the action and we were so close, I could smell the liniment on the players' legs! It was very exciting and the whole game passed in what seemed like 15 minutes. My team beat Rotherham 6-1 and there I was, thinking my new-found team would always win by five and I would see two hat tricks. The innocence of youth!

Reflecting as an adult on the statistics from this game, the thing that really strikes me is the size of the crowd, which was under 15,000. Until I researched this book, I always thought the ground was packed to the rafters for this game, but of course, everyone looks big to a 9-year-old!

I asked a few friends about their first games and I recognised many similarities and it's apparent, we really are a football family. See what you think.

Paul, who we call 'Paul the Greek' because we can't pronounce 'Calotychos', also saw his first live football match at the old Dell, in 1976 when Southampton played Manchester City. Don't worry, this isn't another Southampton story and it's an interesting example of how a love for a club can grow in an odd way and then become unshakable. In Paul's first game, Mick Channon was playing for Southampton and young Paul instantly loved his flair and general positive demeanour on the field. Therefore, when Mick Channon was sold to Manchester City in 1977 for £300,000 (which incidentally broke my heart), Paul followed him and became a 'Blue Moon'. Paul's first Manchester City match was again at Southampton in 1979 (he lives in Hampshire) after his dad finally gave in to his nagging. His love affair with City was now consummated and it has lasted ever since for around 40 years. Mick actually came back to Southampton in 1979, but sadly Paul did not!

John is a long-time colleague and friend and Newcastle born and bred, together with that lovely accent. His first game was up north in the arctic cold of St James Park and was Newcastle United versus Crystal Palace on 31st January 1970. He told me he was about 7 years old and taken by his dad. Apparently, he was dropped off at the 'Boys Turnstile' and started the queueing. His dad got in quickly and then stood worrying in the ground for his son, who didn't appear. He needn't have worried, as they were reconnected after a 30-minute wait. Imagine that today – it would have made Crimewatch!

John remembers this first game with his dad vividly. Little Geordie John was so looking forward to his first match and therefore when he arrived home, his mum understandably asked him if it was fun. He told me that he replied to her, "It was a bit boring mum." He then preceded to add, "But, the ball was kicked out of the ground over the stand and then when they restarted play with a new ball, the old ball flew back over the stand and they had TWO balls!" The things children remember and that impress them!

As is often the case when supporting a team, it doesn't always go as planned, because it also finished in a goal-less draw and John, I'm afraid you can't blame Mike Ashley for that!

Our son in law Jon was born and bred in Norwich, before leaving East Anglia to spread his wings (included netting our eldest daughter Natalie and giving us two lovely grandchildren). He recalled to me how his first game was just about as memorable as you could get and was possibly one of his team's most famous matches of all time (well, in East Anglia), when they were drawn against their bitter rivals Ipswich Town (see more on this rivalry in Chapter 4). This was the semi-final of the Milk Cup (which is now known as the League Cup, if you ignore the marketing branding). It was a two-legged affair and in the first game at Portman Road, Jon's team lost 1-0. It was all set for

Jon's first match in the second leg on 6th March 1985. It was apparently a birthday present for 9 year old Jon and don't you agree, what a great present for a young lad? Better still for Jon, Norwich came from behind to win 2-0 and 2-1 on aggregate and reach the final at Wembley (which they won). Jon's first game was at a Carrow Road capacity crowd of 23,545. Without our 9 year old birthday boy, it would have been 23,544 and I'm sure he played his role in this great Canary event!

All these years later, Jon recalled to me being in total awe at the size of the crowd, the noise and the excitement and remembers simply sitting there wide-eyed and just gazing around – basically star struck. Understandably, he was hooked, but as with most of our teams, it rarely gets back to these highs after that, but you can't tell an excited 9 year old birthday boy this; and as stated in this chapter title, no going back after that!

Stuart is a friend and colleague who also comes from East Anglia, but is born and bred, wait for it – in Ipswich! As a young boy, he must have watched in horror at his team's demise against Norwich and doesn't that just explain so clearly that there are two sides to every football experience. All the more reason to not let the football get in the way!

Stuart is a passionate Ipswich Town fan who travels all over the country following his team and his own first match was Ipswich versus Middlesbrough on 23rd April 1977 and as is so often the case, he was taken by his dad. Back in the 1970s Ipswich Town were one of England's finest teams, regularly at the top of the league. Therefore, as a 9 year old, Stuart told me his expectations were high as Ipswich won most home games they played. Unfortunately, Stuart was to learn at an early age that football doesn't always go as planned and his team lost 1-0 at home to Middlesbrough and a David Armstrong goal.

Around the coast in the heart of the East End of London, with my long-time friend and business colleague Alan, we find a different story and

Alan told me how he had to bear the pain of unfrequented love, with his West Ham passion. Apparently, when schoolboy Alan and his family lived in the East End of London, Alan's mum banned her boys from going to West Ham because it was 'too rough' and instead preferred them walking through the Woolwich Tunnel to Charlton. Of course, they obeyed her and it was only when Alan was aged 21 and the family had moved from London, that he told me that he felt able to see his first West Ham match. Despite this difficult start, Alan and his whole family chose West Ham and sadly, Charlton lost a few lifelong passionate fans!

I have had similar and wonderful first game experiences introducing and taking my two grandsons to their first games when seven and eight years old respectively. The look in their eyes of awe and wonder reminded me so much of my own first match and those that clearly happened in Newcastle, Norwich and Ipswich.

Do you see a trend here as all these years later these fellow fans teams haven't changed at all?

Do you remember your first game and who took you along?

You have heard of mine and a few friends' first games and I bet your own was memorable as well.

For me, after 27th April 1964 and Rotherham United, I was hooked and there was no going back, so bring on the passion, pleasure and it has to be said; pain!

Chapter 2

They Were Tin Shacks, But We Loved Them!

Now-a-days when I go to football grounds they are, almost without exception, excellent, modern stadiums with great facilities and TV screens in the concourses.

I haven't been to every ground in the Premier League, but do aim to achieve this, that is all the time my team stays up long enough to allow me to achieve this goal! However, I do still have a yearning for those football grounds from previous eras, that let's just say, were not perfect!

Swindon Town's ground, the County Ground is just such an old school ground. I had some enjoyable trips there when my team were in League One (apart from the brick through our supporters' coach window). Rather than wreak revenge on my behalf, my friend and colleague Stuart showed the caring side of football fans when his team Ipswich visited Swindon Town. He told me that as he and his friends walked along the road to Swindon's game before the match, they heard someone from above forlornly calling, "Can you help me?"

They looked up and there was a man who had been cleaning his windows up a ladder, stuck on a small parapet. Apparently, the ladder had fallen away and he was dangerously stranded above ground. Being good practical Tractor Boys, they proceeded to help him carefully come down, until falling the last six feet into their collective arms.

What a story and I have a hunch that this would never happen at Old Trafford, not because Northern fans are cold hearted, but because no-one would be so mad as to clean their windows on match day near Old Trafford!

I really loved my own team's old ground and in fact, its enormous imperfections were its charm. We all really had two grounds; the pre-Hillsborough ground and the all-seater ground after 1995. Quite frankly, all around the country, the all-seater grounds were a shadow of their former selves, but they were undoubtedly safer.

When my team's old ground was a 30,000 capacity standing ground, it was a beast and especially to the away teams who hated its intimacy and rustic authenticity. When it rocked, it was raucous, raw and in your face and that's why, as home fans, we loved it!

Before all seating, grounds were crammed full of fans and I remember my late brother taking me to a game against Fulham after work, which we had to run to get into and then cram into the back of the open stand and slowly push our way to a reasonable view of the pitch over the first 10 minutes. The away fans were pushed into a cage to the left, like penned wild animals.

It wasn't nice, but over the years, I did see a few away fans act just like wild animals (and some home fans as well, to be fair)!

With the pitch being above the bottom of the terraces and the touchline so close to the wall, it was hell for visiting players, especially full backs. Every time they bent down to pick up the ball for a throw in, they were subjected to a tirade of abuse, right next to their face. I sometimes felt sorry for them, but not for long! No wonder they didn't like playing at the old grounds and often being narrow pitches, that didn't help either.

I have seen opposing full backs, literally freeze or even lose it and get sent off, goaded by the home fans. Under floodlights was the best and these games could create quite an atmosphere.

I know fans of other clubs would say exactly the same about their own grounds and quite frankly it was true of many old school grounds, but less so now-a-days, with so many modern stadiums and overseas ticket sales and corporate influences covered more in Chapter 14. It definitely feels that now-a-days home advantage is not as critical as previously. It's why we all love it when a big club gets drawn away at a non-league team in the FA Cup.

Upton Park was a great stadium and always created a fabulous atmosphere that was very intimidating for away teams and fans alike. I remember sitting in the Bobby Moore stand as an intruder away fan and my team scoring in the last minute to effectively relegate West Ham. If I had so much as smiled, I would have been pummelled and I would have deserved it – I shouldn't have been there!

Luton Town's old ground at Kenilworth Road was a classic old school stadium (I use this term 'stadium' with caution) and I remember being caged behind the goal and when my team scored, falling down six terrace steps with excitement. The pies were good too!

Son-in-law Jon says of his club's ground Carrow Road that it's a lovely old ground and he is very fond of it. I have stayed at the hotel on the corner of the ground on match day and that was a great experience. Some grounds feel welcoming and friendly and, in my opinion, Carrow Road is still one such ground.

Goodison Park to this day retains this old school feeling and how will things change negatively for Everton if they move to a new modern stadium? White Hart Lane was another classic old school ground and as covered earlier, I suffered personally there, although Spurs' new ground was carefully planned for acoustics and atmosphere and is a magnificent arena.

Do you have similar warm feelings about your old or existing ground?

We have reflected on how strong our passion for our own team is once smitten, but do you have another football team where you have a bit of a soft spot for them and their fans and I don't mean a 'second team'? Mine is Crystal Palace and some memorable away days at Sellhurst Park.

I think the reason I have a soft spot for Palace is firstly, because they are not a 'big club' (I mean not a Top Six club) and most of their supporters either live in South London or have roots in South London. It also helps that they feel like an authentic club, enhanced by good old Sellhurst Park itself. It's a balanced soft spot too, as not all my memories of away days there are positive results!

Little things like the eagle flying cross-pitch before the game and the Dave Clarke Five song 'Glad All Over' that they adapted with the banging on the tin at the back of the stand, all help with this feeling that Crystal Palace are a 'proper club' with 'proper supporters.' I even like their whacky, if slightly annoying Ultras in black jackets who started in England, all the drums and European style chants.

On 13th January 1973, my team played at Crystal Palace in the third round of the cup. I was aged 18 and with several friends we decided to follow the team up to South London. This was a British Rail Special Train outing and as usual, we drank and played cards all the way to Crystal Palace station. Once the game started, my team was taken apart by Don Rogers and lost 2-0, but it could have been much worse. The crowd was 31,604 which is a testament to how seriously the FA Cup was taken back then (see more in Chapter 3). However, the real drama was on the way home.

On the train back home, we all sat quietly disappointed at our team's poor display (nothing new there) and opposite us on a seat was a young lad of about our age, who was clearly very drunk. He was on his own and had obviously become separated from his friends, red in the face and quite slurringly inebriated. We were travelling at speed back to Hampshire and the train had no stops until home, so was probably going at 100 miles an hour.

Our well-oiled friend obviously urgently needed some air and moved to the door where he pulled down the window to get some fresh oxygen into his battered body - nothing too exciting yet. Unfortunately, when he leant on the window the door opened and the rush of air blew the door all the way open. Right next to my face, looking IN at me from the outside, whilst travelling at 100 miles an hour and clinging on for dear life, was our drunk friend. For maybe 10 seconds this continued, but it seemed like a full minute.

Thankfully, we went around a corner and the wind blew him back in and the door slammed shut. Our friend sat back in his seat, now white faced and VERY quiet. Strangely, none of us said a thing to him, as were all so terrified and it was a shocking experience to see someone come so close to certain death. The lad would now be in his mid-sixties and if you are reading this now, I guess you know exactly who you are and that this was you. Let me sincerely say now, "I'm so glad you survived" as it saved me a fortune in subsequent post-traumatic stress counselling fees!

I have been to Sellhurst Park on quite a few occasions and sometimes my team lost and occasionally my team won, but I have always enjoyed the away day at Palace. There really is something about the club, its supporters and its ground that are authentic in an old school way and I like it!

No doubt the owners will build a new ground, the eagle will get banned due to health and safety reasons, the Ultras will dissolve and they will sell more corporate boxes - but for now, it's for real and reminds me of the old days. The grounds from the 1960s, 1970s and 1980s were very basic and of course in England we suffered two tragedies at Hillsborough and Bradford, so physically things had to improve, mainly for safety issues. No-one should ever die at a football game.

In many cases, the grounds were just tin shacks and the urinals were appalling. When a goal was scored, you were pushed or fell five steps down and smoke filled the air everywhere. It was hard core and grass roots, but things did need to change.

A few years ago, my team were relegated right down to League One and without doubt the best part of this, apart from winning a lot more games than normal, was getting the chance to visit many smaller and homelier grounds. When I look back on those League One adventures, one game that particularly highlights the grass roots (or muddy) nature of this level, was an away game with Wycombe Wanderers on a cold and misty Tuesday night!

I loved the raw nature of these types of games in League One. Wycombe wasn't far and so a decision was made to drive up to the game some of us to meet by the ground's burger van (it seemed, the only burger van there). Adams Park holds 9,617 and the away stand, the Hillbottom Stand holds 2,053 and my team's fans crammed that stand full that night. However, the crowd that evening was only 6,232 and therefore I make it only 4,179 home fans - they knew something, we didn't!

It was a typical winter February night, misty and very cold and another key factor in all this, were the Wasps. Not the risk of being stung by some out of season climate change freak bees, but by Wasps Aviva Premier League RFU outfit, who as well as Wycombe Wanderers, played at Adams Park between 2002 and 2014. As a result, the pitch was a disgrace and a mixture of thick mud and heavy sand, but very little grass! It reminded me of going back to the 1970s and grounds like Derby County's Baseball Ground in their 1st Division championship winning season. When the players were warming-up, they couldn't use the centre of the pitch, because it was too muddy and we knew then that this would be fun. My team's goalkeeper and the goalkeeping coach were kicking long to each other and the ball was literally dying in a splodge; it was hilarious.

More was to come though and in my team in 2009-10 we had the very young raw talent of Michail Antonio, who went on to do so well at West Ham. In those days Michail hadn't 'beefed-up' and was slight and primarily a very tricky, fast winger and we loved him with his endless, ball at feet, dribbles. Once the game started, it became very evident that Adams Park post Wasps use, was not the place for tricky dribbles by wafer thin teenage wingers. Twice in the first five minutes Michail ran down the line at speed and left the ball behind in the mud, whilst he kept going five yards on without the ball! It was hilarious and after 32 minutes, Alan Pardew substituted this exciting, rapid talent and replaced him with the not rapid, or exciting, or young, but unique Paul Wotton.

This very sound substitution said it all about this level in the football world. The game was just as you would have expected, a boring, few chances 0-0 draw, but we loved it at Wycombe, because it was like going back in a time machine, the home fans were friendly and it was genuinely old school.

Another similar game was away to Bristol Rovers. The away fans were housed behind the goal and to the side on open terracing. I was sat in a temporary stand, like they erect at County Shows and we were protected from the showers by being under tarpaulin - I jest not! If I recall, it was this game where the away fans had me giggling with a very amusing chant. At Bristol Rovers, the tongue in cheek chant from those under the tarpaulin was, "We're the dry end, we're the dry end, we're the dry end over here." To which those on the uncovered terraces at the side replied, "We're the wet end, we're the wet end, we're the wet end over here!" It was spontaneous and could only happen in

League One and Two. If you experience this every single week, I envy you – honestly.

Of course, Manchester City were not always the powerhouse Big Six team they are now and in the late 1990s Paul the Greek travelled around the country visiting many lower league games. He reflects that these times were among the best in his football supporting career, with much fun and laughter and of course self-deprecating black humour that genuine football fans do so well.

The appeal of grass roots football in the lower leagues is considerable and one factor that attracts, is the ability to just turn up for a game and not have to buy online in an interminable queue. No seats to choose, no membership number to input and no credit card details to enter and pay online.

Walsall away on 1st March 2011 was another example for me of the absolute grass roots nature and charm of lower leagues football. It was a totally impulsive and last-minute decision to go, which adds to the experience. The journey up to the Midlands was smooth (we were lucky, as we had cut it very tight to leave) and we arrived in time for food and drinks. If you haven't been to Walsall's ground, it's the one you can see from the M6 and is a mixture of old and new. It's called the Banks Stadium and holds 11,500 fans and you can park in a field car park, right by the ground - another benefit!

We walked the 250 yards from the car park to go in search of food and drink, but this was answered in one solution when a Walsall steward saw our colours and came up to us and said, "We have opened up our Social Club for you guys tonight, as there are so many of you; you can go in there and they are doing hotdogs and burgers and you can buy yourself some beers." He wasn't joking either, they had opened the main area of the Social Club to welcome the away fans and it was packed. The food was freshly cooked and excellent and there was a happy bubbly atmosphere in the Social Club. It felt really old school and was like Whitchurch United Social Club on a Saturday night in the 1970s!

It was lively, fans mixed and needless-to-say there was no trouble at all. It was very friendly and there was an extremely welcoming feeling throughout. The burgers weren't bad either. This all reflected what is so great about the lower leagues (other than of course, that brick through our supporters' coach window at Swindon).

When you go to grounds such as Arsenal and the Emirates, there is no doubt it's a magnificently impressive stadium. You get significantly more leg room, the seats are soft and it's a 'stadium', not a 'football ground.' However, the atmosphere is generally poor, as you can only hear those fans within 30 yards of you. In the away end at Arsenal, you cannot hear anything else. Walsall's Banks Stadium ('stadium', they are clearly trying to be a Big Six club) is not the Emirates and strangely, I know what I prefer!

The downsides of the lower leagues are indisputable and we had them both that night in bucket loads. Sometimes the grounds can be lacking in facilities and in our stand, it was hard to view the match properly and 'seeing the action', really is a pre-requisite of watching football matches. We had a huge pillar in front of us, which guaranteed that at some stage you missed something and when the ball went high, it went out of sight!

The other problem, as with most League One and League Two pitches, especially as the season wears on, was the poor pitch. This night, Walsall's pitch was well sanded and bobbled in both the grassy and sandy areas, well everywhere really! Even Messi, would have found it tough, let alone my team's League One players. My team lost, but we only had to walk 250 yards to the car and were home by 11.45 p.m. All in all, despite my team's defeat, we were glad we decided to go to Walsall, as it was a typical League One away day and an enjoyable grass roots football experience.

"Do you fancy going to Walsall?" Yes, every time - nice people and a great trip.

Chapter 3

The Magic of the FA Cup

One of the saddest things about modern football is the diminished status of the FA Cup. Every time a Top Six club fields a reserve team when they play away at a Championship side, it just says everything about where the FA Cup sits today in the elite hierarchy and these top club's attitude to the FA Cup.

For most of my football supporting career, the FA Cup was a great competition and truly contained a magical appeal. I know the BBC try really hard to uplift the FA Cup's current status and I applaud this, but in reality, it isn't what it was in times past.

In my childhood in the early 1960s, people still talked about the first Wembley final of 1923 and the estimated crowd of 200,000 and the historic White Horse pictured below.

Not to forget the equally legendary Matthews final of 1953 when Blackpool beat Bolton Wanderers 4-3 and the total irony of Stan Mortenson scoring a Wembley hat trick and yet getting overshadowed in the annals of history. Not fair is it and maybe it would have been fairer to call it, 'The Stan's Final'?

In February 2010, the boots worn by Stanley Matthews in the match were auctioned at Bonhams for £38,400 and in November 2014 Matthews' winning medal was sold for £220,000. The match ball itself fetched £5,250 in 2018. This is not going to happen to the Manchester City 2019 winners' medals – there are too many of them!

Then there was the memorable 1956 final where Manchester City's Bert Trautman broke his neck in goal and yet still carried on, with his team beating Birmingham City 3-1. I feel much sympathy for you Birmingham City fans, getting to an FA Cup final that is touted as an epic final in history and yet no-one ever remembers you were there!

Not to forget the Spurs double in 1961 and its mammoth achievement and yet today Manchester City win everything and its expected! That's also true of 1923, because all anyone remembers is a damn horse, not that Bolton and West Ham were there! Do I sense a trend here of Bolton Wanderers being participators at major sporting events, but never being remembered?

Everton versus Sheffield Wednesday in 1966 was special with Everton winning 3-2 and the overweight Scouser running on the pitch when Everton scored the winner and being rugby tackled by two fit policemen. I watched this as an 11 year old and was absolutely enthralled. In those days the TV coverage on both ITV and BBC started at 10.00 a.m. and ran through until 5.30 p.m. and as a young lad who was mad on football, I watched all seven and a half hours, other than to occasionally leave the screen to kick a ball around outside, against our back wall.

The 1970 final between Chelsea and Leeds United was one of my personal favourite cup finals, being played a on a mud field only a week after the Horse of the Year event. The match finished 2-2 and the replay at Old Trafford the Wednesday following, was an epic game with Chelsea winning 2-1 and the great Peter Osgood scoring the winner with a diving header. That winner was one of those times, when although not a fan of the actual team scoring, it's just so exhilarating, you impulsively jump out of your chair anyway. Do you remember games where you were a neutral, but still instinctively jumped out of your seat at a goal?

We had two of the biggest cup final upsets in the 1970s with Sunderland beating Leeds United 1-0 and Jim Montgomery making that amazing save to deny Leeds and of course, my team Southampton beating Manchester United 1-0 with Bobby Stokes, born and bred in Portsmouth, scoring and thank goodness we didn't have VAR then!

It's also not widely known, but when West Ham beat Arsenal 1-0 in 1980, they were in the Second Division, so that meant three Second Division teams winning in 7 years. That would never happen today!

In 1978 Ipswich Town beat Arsenal 1-0 and won the FA Cup for the first and so far, only time. Ipswich fan and friend Stuart was aged 11 at the time and watched the match at his aunties. In fact, at this early age, Stuart was displaying a level of football passion we can all understand and respect. Stuart told me that his young sister was an excellent dancer back then and by chance, was performing at the Royal Albert Hall on cup final day.

Of course, this was a big deal for the family. Stuart's mum and dad went to the Royal Albert Hall and for his part, Stuart watched wall to wall football and celebrated as his team enjoyed their big day at Wembley. Good man (or boy, as he was) Stuart! Understandably, Stuart feels that the FA Cup meant something then and indeed, it did.

In 1981 Ricky Vilas scored that incredible winner against Manchester City for Spurs in their 3-2 replay win and that was another jump out of your seat moment. For Paul the Greek, the City fan, it wasn't so great, although one silver lining was that despite attending the first drawn game at Wembley, his mum wouldn't let him go to the replay, "Because it was a school night". Well done Mum, you saved your son so much heartache!

How things can change on a dime, as in the 1983 final between Manchester United and Brighton, at 2-2, Gordon Smith of Brighton missed an open goal when one on one in the last minute. Needless-to-say, United won the replay 4-0 and that was Brighton's big moment gone. In 1987 Coventry beating Spurs 3-2 was memorable and remains Coventry's own big moment, so spare a thought for Brighton fans, it could all have been so different for them.

Wimbledon's crazy gang win over Liverpool 1-0 in the following year was their one big moment and they then ended up in Milton Keynes before reforming as AFC Wimbledon, so who knows what might happen after an FA Cup final win!

The magic of the cup is OK if you are not on the receiving end, but although Geordie John was a little too young to view non-league Hereford beating his beloved Newcastle United and Malcom McDonald 2-1 on a bog, he told me that he is fed-up to the back teeth at watching re runs of Ronnie Radford's equaliser from 30 yards to set-up the extra time win, that occurs every year at FA Cup Road Three stage!

This was also true for son and law Jon and his trip to Hillsborough for Norwich City's FA Cup semi-final against Sunderland on 5th April 1992. Norwich were in the First Division and Sunderland in the Second Division, so Norwich were clear favourites.

At the time Robert Fleck was Norwich's best player and a regular goal scorer, but unfortunately, he was injured prior to the semi-final. Apparently, there was a major push to get him fit for Norwich's big game and the local newspapers were full of stories of Robert sitting in an oxygen tent to recover. In full support, all Norwich held its breath!

Therefore, imagine the relief on the coach that Jon and his mates were travelling in on route to the game, when it was announced on the radio that Robert Fleck was playing. Jon says the Canary Lads erupted into cheering. This is the problem with football though. A league above your opponents, your star player back, a huge game, massive expectation, enormous excitement and then reality sets in!

The reality that transpired for Jon and his friends was simple; a terrible game, awful Norwich performance, Robert Fleck not match-fit, a 1-0 loss and that terrible flat disappointment when the oxygen goes out of your balloon. We have all been there Jon and we feel for you, apart of course, from Tractor Boy Stuart!

Our son Tristan remembers a particular FA Cup match at Stamford Bridge between Chelsea and Liverpool which he attended that he told me, he feels was the start of all the great things and subsequent successes at Chelsea. It was 26th January 1997 and a 4th Round tie. Liverpool were an excellent side with the Spice Boys in full flow and were 2-0 up at half time through Robbie Fowler and Stan Collymore and Tristan says it could easily have been four or five. Then at half time they brought on Mark Hughes who started to bully Liverpool and second half goals from Hughes, Zola and two by Gianluca Vialli gave Chelsea a wildly exciting win. Chelsea went on to win the FA Cup that season and then the European Cup Winners Cup the next season and the rest is history.

Isn't it strange how at 2-0 the third goal is so important? Once you get back to 2-1, all the momentum changes. The game finished 4-2 and after the match, Tristan told me that the Chelsea fans were going crazy and climbing up trees and no doubt you can recall some of your own team's big cup wins and how you celebrated, I hope, not by climbing trees! Understandably, Tristan also reflects that in those days, the FA Cup mattered and teams played their first teams, even in the Fourth Round.

My own team have reached only two FA Cup finals in modern times (to date of course, as I live in hope) and the final on 1st May 2976 we won and the second FA Cup Final was in 2003 – which I missed!

When you don't support a BIG Club, your team rarely gets to major finals and when they do, it's special. The reason I missed the FA Cup Final on 17th May 2003 against Arsenal at Cardiff was simple and powerful; our eldest daughter Natalie got married to her husband Jon. When her and her future husband Jon told us of the date for their wedding, it was 16 months out and we put it in our diaries and of course, I didn't even work out it was FA Cup Final day.

I certainly didn't expect my team to reach the Cup Final, as after all my team have only done this once before since 1903 - the odds were in my favour! It was after the quarter final game, that I checked out the Cup Final date and immediately knew that if my team made it to the final, I couldn't go.

To make matters worse, they had booked a hotel for the wedding, which shall be nameless, but was quite close to Portsmouth!

Therefore, it transpired that I was on my feet giving my 'Father of the Bride' speech, whilst my team were on the field at Cardiff losing to Arsenal. On the day of Natalie's wedding, I gave one of the waiters a few pounds to keep me up-to-date on the score, which he did. However, he was clearly a Pompey fan and told me the final score with some relish - but still took my money! More importantly, the wedding was a great success and everyone enjoyed the occasion.

Strangely, when you lose a big game like this, it's sometimes better not to experience it first-hand. To this day, I have never watched the recordings of this final or even the goal. Well, that's what I have told myself over the years, to ease my pain. There is little more important in life than your 'Little Princess' getting married to the man she loves and this really was the ultimate 'no-brainer' choice.

However, I have heard of many people going to crazy lengths to get to their team's big final. People fly in from Australia, people get married in the morning and turn up at Wembley in their wedding attire.

Did you ever miss just such an occasion with your team, where it was literally unavoidable? If you did, I feel for you.

I'm sorry if I missed covering your own team's FA Cup glories, but without a doubt and despite my omission, that moment is ensconced in your memory and will never be lost. The FA Cup really had magic and isn't it sad, this seems mainly now lost forever?

Chapter 4

Those Bitter Rivalries

My own team's is Portsmouth FC, or Pompey, as they are known. Who are yours?

I mean of course, your bitter rivals. Typically, these will be your local rivals, but not always. Sometimes these rivalries can develop into wild hatreds although personally, I much prefer hyper competitive banter over hatred.

In this chapter we look at some of the country's more memorable rivalries and even read what it feels like to be on both sides of the rivalry. It does appear that every team has at least one rival, so as football fans, we clearly enjoy this aspect of our passion.

I'm going to be slightly controversial now and I apologise if it isn't in accord with your own deep-rooted beliefs, but I don't want to hate anyone, especially someone from a team down the road, who I have never met. In my view, as in life, you get good and bad in all groups and in any event, at least Portsmouth FC fans passionately support their local club.

Personally, I respect this and have more disrespect for those living in Portsmouth walking around in Top Six shirts. It's just my personal view and I know it's not common amongst many fans. Hopefully, I haven't offended anyone with what I write.

Our son Tristan who is also an author of children's reading books and a Primary School teacher told me that his line with the children, is to recommend to them that they don't too easily use the word 'hate', as when we hate something, we don't want it to exist anymore. That's a harsh wish, isn't it?

Imagine life without your bitter rivals; you may dislike them, but life would be less fun and interesting, if they didn't exist. Strangely, I think if we could wish away our rivals, we would just find another replacement bitter rival!

Many of my own team's fans have a tribal discord that can and does sway towards hatred of Portsmouth FC and as far as I can gather, it's mutual. It does provide some enjoyable 'banter' and plenty of anti-rival songs, plus Social Media jokes (again completely reciprocated). This rivalry runs deep and goes back a long time, but unfortunately, I sense the tribalism is getting worse.

It wasn't always this bad, as my dad would sometimes watch Pompey as well as my team, as did plenty of his friends and this would be unheard of in modern times. Such is the potential for trouble, that when my team do play them, it's a 12.00 p.m. kick off and away fans get herded in and out in a 'vacuum.' Unfortunately, the vacuum doesn't always hold!

My first local derby against my team's rivals was away on 6th February 1966 when my school friend Dylan's dad took us to Fratton Park. Although there was sporadic aggressive behaviour, it was mild compared to today and obviously seemed safe enough to take two 11 year olds.

Typically, fans of clubs with rivals have an urban myth to confirm why their bitter rivalry is justified. The Southampton-Portsmouth rivalry may be part urban myth and part reality, but it apparently goes back centuries and beyond football and usually involved each city's maritime heritage. It is said that when the Titanic sank in 1912, that sailors from Southampton refused to crew her sister ship Olympic because of insufficient numbers of lifeboats, but really this was a beef with the owners, not the port of Portsmouth. However, it is said (although I'm not sure how much of this is fact) that dockers from Portsmouth replaced their Southampton counterparts.

Much of the rivalry centred on competition for port use, one wholly commercial (Southampton) and one-armed forces (Portsmouth). In the early part of the twentieth century, Southampton and Portsmouth dockers would regularly travel along the coast to each other's port for work and in difficult economic times, competition was fierce. Of course, Pompey fans use the union's acronym from the early twentieth century as a derogatory term for Saints fans.

However, despite the mutual unpleasantness, my dad told me that when Southampton was blitzed by German bombers in the Second World War, fire fighters from Portsmouth risked life and limb to extinguish the flames and I'm sure it would be the same now if, god forbid, either city had a major terrorist attack. This tribalism really can be rather stupid. Just my opinion though.

What's your team's bitter rivalry and what is the urban myth to justify its origins?

In modern times, someone playing for an away team, who once played for your bitter rivals, is roundly abused for 90 minutes, every time he touches the ball and it's the same the other way around. But surely, they are just professionals and will play where they are paid? They are not like us, it's just a job, so our booing is wasted really. I'm sure you have indulged in this pantomime booing yourself – I have.

West Ham seem to have a special nuance for angry rivalries. As far as I can tell, Hammers fans strongly dislike Chelsea and have a particularly angry place in their hearts for Spurs. I went as a guest of friend Alan to a West Ham versus Chelsea game once and in the pub near the ground before hand, I swear anyone coming in with a Chelsea shirt on would have been instantly and violently set upon. It was a hot headed and powder keg atmosphere. Anyone going to Stamford Bridge for the reverse fixture, I'm sure would have experienced something similar, in reverse.

Of course, West Ham fan's intense dislike of Millwall is legendary and has often expressed itself in significantly violent events. The feeling is mutual and in 1976 this tragically led to the death of a Millwall supporter and in 2009 at a West Ham v Millwall fixture all hell let loose with widespread fighting and disorder. Originally both teams were only 3 miles apart and the Metropolitan Police must pray each year that Millwall FC don't get promoted to the Premier League (or West Ham get relegated, of course)!

Let's explore some of the more well-known rivalries across the country and start with Spurs/Arsenal, which as an outsider, generally doesn't appear to involve hatred, but is just hyper-competitive, but no doubt some Spurs, or Arsenal fans would disagree. Liverpool/Everton appears very similar and you virtually never hear of fighting at Merseyside Derbies and I understand some families in Liverpool have members who support both teams.

In Scotland the Celtic/Rangers rivalry is legendary and made especially bitter because so much of it is based upon religious leanings. I haven't been to an Old Firm derby but have it up there on my own personal bucket list.

Probably one of the most bitter rivalries in England is Manchester United and Liverpool and this one really is extreme and one that has been heightened in the Premier League era. Aston Villa and Birmingham have a particularly fierce rivalry, coming as they do from the same city and this often overflows into violence. The Sheffield derby seems fairly passionate, as does the Manchester derby, but neither obviously outrageously angry, but I could be wrong. Sunderland/Newcastle seems pretty fierce.

Now, let's look at the tongue-in-cheek named 'Old Farm' rivalry between East Anglian teams Norwich City and Ipswich Town, but this time from both sides. In this case I have a unique opportunity knowing Jon from Norwich and Stuart from Ipswich. Perception really is reality, so let's see what a Norwich fan says about their rivals Ipswich and then what an Ipswich fan says about Norwich. This should be interesting!

When I asked son in law Jon, Norwich born and bred and proud of it, what he thought of Ipswich Town, he said; "They are our rivals, that's for sure. I'm not the type of person to say I hate them or anyone. I do laugh though when they are struggling and I always remember when we weren't in a great financial position, at the same time as Ipswich having a new owner and their fans coming to Carrow Road and waving £20 notes around to mock us. I have to admit they have more history than us and have won the First Division title and a European tournament. I bet many of their fans would say we aren't actually their rivals, suggesting they are too big for that! I always look out for the Ipswich score straight after the Norwich score and I know that's sad, but I bet Ipswich fans do the same and if so, I understand this; but I don't hate them, just have some fun with the rivalry."

When I asked friend and colleague Stuart, who is Ipswich born and bred and proud of it, what he thought of Norwich City, he said; "I actually see Colchester as our main rivals! Three major trophies to nil, enough said. I have to admit that they (Editor's Note – he means Norwich, not Colchester) have caught up a bit over the last few years and are doing OK now. Despite this, I feel we will always be their footballing superiors! Plus of course, Delia used to support us, before Norwich (Editor note; 'allegedly')! Seriously though, football heh, it can be tough. Our fixture list in League One started with Burton Albion (A), Sunderland (H) and Peterborough (A) and I thought to myself that this looked a tough start. How things can change, with Norwich playing Liverpool and Chelsea in their first four matches."

Which they will change again Stuart, but for the better, just be patient and enjoy regularly winning a few more games down in League One – I loved it there.

Now reader, that was interesting wasn't it? In my opinion, Jon and Stuart are both fair, reasonable, intelligent and articulate men, born and bred in East Anglia and proud of their heritage. Did you notice they both say virtually the same things, but with a strongly biased perspective? It appears that rivalries work for us all, on both sides of the divide? The biggest things we have in common are our love of football and our passion for our team. Dare I say that it seems to me that Jon and Stuart are almost identical but don't tell them, I won't. Oohps, I just did!

These rivalries inevitably develop tribal songs, some of which are quite unpleasant and not able to be relayed here, but you know what they are! Then of course we have the derogatory nicknames. Portsmouth fans refer to my team's fans as Stains (an extremely complex anagram of Saints) or Scummers. In return Pompey fans are Skates (an unpleasant fishy smell). Newcastle fans refer to Sunderland fans as Mackems and this is interesting. It was used to describe the making of ships - "We mack em". Since it started being used, people from Sunderland have understandably taken pride in describing themselves as Mackems and their shipbuilding heritage. But on Tyneside, it has become a derogatory phrase, especially when football fans try to poke fun at their rivals. Perception really is reality when it comes to football rivalries!

These rivalries are not just local either. What about Crystal Palace and Brighton and Hove Albion, which seems a particularly fierce rivalry and yet the teams are 41 miles apart and that M23/A23 on a bad day of traffic, can take two and a half hours. That's hardly just down the road!

Leeds and Manchester United is another very aggressive rivalry and these teams live 45 miles apart, but this probably has more to do with the Lancashire/Yorkshire rivalry which of course goes right back to the War of The Roses from 1445 to 1485.

Football rivalries are not limited to just the more well known, as many non-Premier League teams have their own unique local rivals. How about these to add to the list; Derby-Notts Forest, Stoke-Port Vale,

Bristol Rovers-Bristol City, Blackburn-Burnley, Cardiff-Swansea, Chester-Wrexham, Luton-Watford, Hereford-Shrewsbury, Oxford-Swindon and more?

I apologise if I have missed your own bitter rivalry, but you know what it is, don't you and now is a good time to snarl at the thought of your bitter rivals?

Finally, I think it says it all about these bitter rivalries, that there is always big trouble when Exeter play Plymouth down on the beautiful South Devon coast, where you would have thought those living in this warm, palm tree lined location, would at least be chilled-out enough to stay calm!

Chapter 5

Some People Think It's Kenneth Wolstenholme

30th July 1966 was the most memorable day so far in English football history and I was 11 years old at the time and I consider myself lucky to have been able to experience this quite incredible national experience.

It was of course, the day that England won the football World Cup for the first and at the time of writing, only time. Later in Chapter 7 we reflect on the host of nearly moments for the English national team, but on 30th July 1966, it WAS that moment!

The tournament was held in England for the first and only time so far and the country experienced great anticipation. Our first game was against Uruguay and it finished goalless and you could sense the collective deflation of the country after this disappointment.

Next up was Mexico and at last a win by 2-0 with a stunning longshot from Bobby Charlton that changed the nation's luck. Then another 2-0 win over France and we were through to the knock-out stages.

I was able to stay up to watch the evening game against Mexico, even if it was a school night. Live football on TV was rare then, so the growing excitement in the country was palpable. In those days the round after the group stages was the quarter finals. It was all we could talk about at school the next morning.

On Saturday 23rd July 1966 England played Argentina at Wembley in the World Cup quarter final and one of my friends from down the road in our rural council estate was taken by his dad to the match – lucky devil! All these years later, I'm still envious. I need to let this go now!

England won 1-0 with the only goal courtesy of a Geoff Hurst header. During this controversial game Argentina's Antonio Rattin became the first player to be sent off in a senior international football match at Wembley. At first, he refused to leave the field and eventually had to be escorted off by several policemen. In Argentina, this game is called 'el robo del sigl'o' (the robbery of the century); bless, although of course their pay-back hand ball robbery of us was to still come in 1986!

The tournament was all going so fast and we were in the semi-finals now. The next big game was a mid-week game against Portugal on 26th July 1966 and were up against the tournament's hero, Eusebio. Two Bobby Charlton goals and one from Eusebio meant we won 2-1 and incredibly, we were in the final.

Now, the country really was obsessed!

Saturday 30th July 1966 was just one of those days. My dad, brother and I sat down all day to enjoy the maddingly exciting spectacle. My mum kept the freshly baked cakes and cups of teas coming. When we went 1-0 down, it just felt so deflating. When we equalised, spirits exploded and when Martin Peters made it 2-1 to us with 12 minutes to go, it felt like the miracle was going to happen.

Now, as a football fan for over 55 years, I have had several traumatic and galling moments, but that German equaliser in the last minute and me being just 11 years old, was too much to cope with. My dad and brother (who was 21 at the time), were devastated. I simply couldn't stand the tension in extra time and just had to retreat to my bedroom and avoid any more disappointment.

I was only eleven, so don't judge me too harshly or think of me as a wimp!

I have no idea what I did for 15 minutes in my bedroom. It's a complete void in my memory bank. I just remember being distressed.

However, what followed, whilst I was in my bedroom goes down in English and worldwide football history as, "One of those moments"!

When Geoff Hurst's shot hit the cross bar and bounced down and was given as a goal, my dad and brother blew the roof off our house (well, figuratively anyway). I stormed down the stairs, but all the way down knew what the noise meant – England were ahead again in the World Cup final.

Thank goodness that there was no VAR in 1966 (we didn't even have a colour TV back then), as I suspect that goal might not have been given in 2019.

As it happens, I missed the most controversial moment in English football history – but heh ho, we won and history was made!

I watched the last 19 minutes with my family, which felt like an age. Alan Ball was magnificent and in the last minute of extra time, Geoff Hurst broke away, some fans ran on the pitch, he smashed it into the roof of the net, England won the World Cup and Kenneth Wolstenholme secured his place in history with the greatest ever commentator's sentence ..."Some people are on the pitch, they think it's all over – it is now" (with perfect timing and pause, before Hurst smashed it in).

We all cried, we hugged and it was memorable. I have never watched a replay of that moment since without getting tears in my eyes and remembering hugging my late dad and late brother at that unforgettable moment. The country went mad and celebrated like never before and football reached a high I haven't seen since.

30th July 1966 was watched in England by approximately 20 million people and my estimate is that there are only a few millions of us left now, so I was lucky. I have since touched the crossbar where Geoff Hurst's shot hit, when enjoyable an official tour of the old Wembley in 1990. That was a unique feeling to rub a piece of special wood!

There is no doubt something quite superb, was made even better by Kenneth Wolstenholme's professional brilliance, so thank you Kenneth

Chapter 6

Mexico 1970 and THAT Stomach Bug!

After 1966, anything seemed possible and in 1970 we so nearly achieved it. England were world champions and therefore didn't have to pre-qualify for the 1970 World Cup in Mexico. At the time I was taking my O Levels (as they were called then), 15 years old and absolutely football mad.

The 1970 World Cup is a difficult memory for me and recently when sorting through some old papers, I found my school report from 1971. In those days, the Headmaster added his comment to the various subject teachers' comments. There, bold as brass was written by the headmaster, "Richard has now passed the O Levels he needs to take his A Levels, which would have happened six months earlier without the World Cup in Mexico."

When reading this some 48 years later, Marion my wife said, "Nothing changes, does it?" I have to say, "It's a fair cop!"

As you can see, I did my bit, so what about the players? In my humble opinion, the 1970 team was even better than the 1966 team. We still had the tactically astute Alf Ramsey as manager, we were super confident and the team included; Gordon Banks, Geoff Hurst, Booby Charlton, Martin Peters, Bobby Moore, Alan Ball, Alan Mullery, Francis Lee, Terry Cooper, Nobby Stiles, Emlyn Hughes, Colin Bell, Peter Osgood, Allan Clarke plus many others. This was an excellent squad of experienced players with three truly world class players (Banks, Moore and Charlton).

We were drawn in the same group as Brazil, although the top two qualified for the quarter finals. The first match was uneventful and on 2nd June 1970 we eased past Rumania 1-0 before the big one on 7th June 1970 against the mighty Brazil. I believe that the Brazilian team of 1970 was the greatest football team I have EVER seen play. They were simply magnificent and what about this list of greats; Pelé, Carlos Alberto, Gérson, Jairzinho, Rivellino and Tostão?

On 7th June 1970, we saw what was probably, the best-ever England team performance against the best-ever team, playing at their best – and we lost! It was football at its peak, played in an incredibly sporting way, in an exotic environment of heat, colour and drama. It does not get better than that match in terms of a spectacle!

This was the match of memorable moments. Booby Moore's incredibly beautiful and clean tackle on Pelé and being applauded for it on the pitch by the great man and possibly the best defender's tackle in history. England hitting the post and Jeff Astle's miss of an open goal (what a shame for him), Brazil's great goal and of course, that stupendous save by Gordon Banks from Pelé, without doubt the best-ever goalkeeper's save in a big game, plus another fantastic commentary by David Coleman, that just added to the experience.

We gave everything we had and just came up short and it really could have gone either way. At the time we felt sad but also proud, because we knew we had watched something very special. Weighing up the colourful environment, the great players playing at their peak, the competitiveness, the importance of the game and the sporting manner in which it was played, it really was the best football game I ever experienced in 55 plus years, despite the fact that we lost!

However, the tournament wasn't over and the next game we beat Czechoslovakia 1-0 and we were off to Leon to play West Germany in the quarter final. Then, something happened that changed football history. Gordon Banks fell 'foul' to a savage stomach bug that meant at the very last minute he couldn't play against West Germany and Peter Bonetti of Chelsea came in for him. Peter was a very good player, but not the world's best goalie who had just made that crazy Pelé save.

There has been much speculation since, that Gordon's food was tampered with, but really in Mexico, one has to say a stomach bug could happen at any time, so I'm not really into these conspiracy theories. However, whatever the reason, it was undeniably damaging to our cause.

It started so well with us going 2-0 up with goals from Mullery and Peters and we were well on top and Dad and I were jumping around the room again (my brother John had moved to Australia by then). In fact, it was going so well that Alf Ramsey substituted Bobby Charlton to save him game time in the blistering Leon heat and get him ready for the forthcoming semi-finals. Oh dear and what a pivotal mistake, that undoubtedly came from over confidence. Taking Bobby Charlton off meant that Franz Beckenbauer was free to go forward and not man-to-man mark our best player and we paid the price for this change.

There were only 22 minutes to go and we were 2-0 up until Beckenbauer and Seeler scored goals that I'm sure Gordon Banks would have saved, but who knows, that may be wishful thinking. There was only going to be one winner in extra time and our deflation was complete. It was horribly difficult to take and when you are 15 years old, you are not best equipped for such disappointments.

My dad as usual was brilliant with his feet well and truly on the ground and the pain was eased a little by the incredible West Germany 3 Italy 4 semi-final and Brazil's absolute annihilation of Italy 4-1 in the final, completed by that incredible Jairzinho goal after so many passes.

We didn't win in Mexico 1970 and in fact lost our two big games, but it was a wonderful spectacle and the best ever team to play football, won the competition, but we came so close to beating this once in a lifetime team.

My overriding memory of Mexico 1970 is one of sadness and pride at the same time and that damn stomach bug - it makes you sick!

Chapter 7

All Those Years and Still Hurting

In 1970 I believed this represented just about my worst England disappointment, but actually I was wrong on so many levels!

There are not so many of us around now that lived through Mexico 1970, but some of the more recent traumas have been shared with many, including my friends. Following the 1970 German disappointment, the next big England trauma I remember was the night of 17th October 1973 when England needed to beat Poland at Wembley to qualify for the World Cup finals in Germany in 1974.

We were in a group of only three; Wales, Poland and England and only drawing at home to Wales and losing in Poland 2-0 in front of 105,000 baying Polish fans, wasn't good. However, despite this, a win at Wembley on 17th October at home to Poland would see us through. Alf Ramsey was still manager, but his powers were waning and many of the greats from his 1966 and 1970 teams were in decline and falling from the team.

The stage was set for a great English win in front of 100,000 at Wembley. TV pundit Brian Clough famously pre-match referred to the Polish goalkeeper Jan Tomaszewski as 'a clown'. We would all live to regret that imprudent and disrespectful comment.

It turned out to be a heart breaking game that was hard to understand. It was a completely one-sided match that saw England take 36 shots to Poland's two, force 26 corners, hit the woodwork twice and have four efforts cleared off the line. We just couldn't score and it felt like we were destined not to win. Norman Hunter (who never made mistakes or missed tackles), lost the ball weakly on the halfway line, they broke, the shot went under Peter Shilton (who never dived over the ball) and we were behind.

It finished 1-1 but we were not at the World Cup finals and it really was hard to take. Newcastle John remembers this as his worst memory in supporting England. Poland did go on to finish third in the subsequent Word Cup, but it was hard to take the morning after that

Wembley night. I still remember the heartache of the bus trip to work the next day.

Little did I know that as a 19 year old, this was just a practice run for future England traumas to come.

We failed to qualify for Argentina 1978, having the same points total in qualifying as Italy, but a worse goal difference, so the disappointment was less extreme than the Poland game and we played well to beat Italy 2-0 at Wembley with Kevin Keegan scoring.

The 1982 World Cup final was disappointing in a whole new way. The tournament was an initial group of four followed by a group of three and we actually managed to play five games and not lose any, but still not qualify for the semi-finals. We had a good team that year, but even that wasn't enough. The tournament for us, culminated with a 0-0 draw with Spain on 5th July 1982 when Trevor Brooking and Kevin Keegan were both injured and not fully fit, but came on as substitutes and both missed glorious chances to score the vital winning goal. England were finding fresh ways to disappoint us all!

On 22nd June 1986 England found a unique and soul-destroying way to lose a big game and get knocked out of the Mexico World Cup. This was of course, 'The Hand of God' day and who would have thought of this way to crush English hopes? I was on holiday in Malta for much of this tournament and had to fly home whilst the match was playing. To that extent, I didn't have to watch live Maradona's blatant cheating with the first goal but have since cringed with rage every time I see it replayed. Yes, his second goal was great, but why couldn't Gary Lineker just get to head in that last minute equaliser?

Although I missed the game, I still managed to be at the airport car park exit hut when the second goal went in, so managed to hear the worst moment, live on the car park attendant's transistor radio. There really was no escape for me from the hurt!

Where were you when it happened?

The 1988 European Championships in West Germany found a new level of disappointment, which was basically play awfully and lose all three games! That will work and it did.

Onto 1990 and the beginning of the 'Penalty Shoot Out Method' to create country-wide trauma. The 1990 World Cup finals were superb with many memorable games and when we reached the semi-final, the whole country was ready for triumph. I'm guessing many of our readers lived through this time and have their own unique memory of that night. Was it just me, or did you just have a feeling of dread that we wouldn't win? There felt such inevitability about the penalty shoot-out failure. I watched it with around twenty of my family and it sort of made the disappointment worse. However, at least we fought well and generally the country was proud. I was devastated, how about you?

17th June 1992 in Sweden at the European Championships was another awful night. We had drawn our first two games nil-nil and when we played the host nation, we were 1-0 up until the second half. Then they equalised and that dreadful Brolin goal that crushed us yet again.

I don't know about you, but I was getting fed-up with this keep happening!

Then, along came another humiliation! In the qualifying group to the 1994 World Cup in the USA, we played Norway away on 2nd June 1993 and lost 2-0 in the famous late Graham Taylor match. Now this wasn't the game where Bjørge Lillelien famously ranted, that was in 1981, but all this game did was re-energise that humiliation, so here goes again; "Lord Nelson, Lord Beaverbrook, Sir Winston Churchill, Sir Anthony Eden, Clement Attlee, Henry Cooper, Lady Diana – Maggie Thatcher can you hear me? Maggie Thatcher ... your boys took a hell of a beating!" Oh dear.

The 1996 European Championships were in England and surely, we had a great chance this time? My son Tristan was now aged 15, so at least I now had someone to share the pain with, although Euro 96 was great, wasn't it? Beating Scotland and that Gascoigne goal, thrashing Holland 4-1 and the Spain penalty shoot-out which incredibly, we won.

However, the pièce de résistance was to come.

We had a great tune, 'Three Lions (Football's Coming Home)' released in 1996 as a single by The Lightning Seeds with the lyrics written by comedians David Baddiel and Frank Skinner and without a doubt it had been 30 Years of Hurt! What we didn't know was that we were to have approaching another 30 years of hurt to come!

The next 30 years of hurt culminated in that penalty shoot-out loss to Germany in the semi-final. The problem with this loss, was that we played so well and were clearly the better team. Somehow, we just

seem destined to lose this way. Tristan and I were devastated and inconsolable. How were you and do you remember where you watched the drama unfound? It was just plain heart breaking, wasn't it?

We weren't finished though, were we? The 1998 World Cup in France found new ways to torture we England fans. This was the World Cup where Glenn Hoddle managed us and we made it to the quarter finals against one of our old enemies, Argentina. No 'Hand of God' this time, but a potential 'Knuckle' by Simeone. Micheal Owen scored that exciting goal and then David Beckham was fouled by Diego Simeone and as Simeone stood up, he allegedly rubbed his knuckles against the back of Beckham's head as Beckham lay face-down on the pitch. Lying on the floor, Beckham quite naturally instinctively swung his leg at

Simeone, after which Simeone fell over poleaxed! The referee then sent Beckham off and we were down to ten men.

Playing like heroes with ten men, England held out against the Argentinian attacks and in the dying moments of the game during a scramble in the Argentine penalty area, Sol Campbell headed the ball into the goal. Given the circumstances, ten men, last minute goal, bitter rivals and a World Cup quarter final, Tristan and I jumped around the room, hollering, hugging and going wild and then out of the corner of our eyes saw that the game was going on and Argentina were attacking.

The referee had disallowed (wrongly) the goal for a foul by Alan Shearer. I believe that moment was the most crestfallen I ever remember feeling in a football game. It felt like we had been sand-bagged. Do you remember where you were when this happened and did you fall 'foul' of similar premature celebration?

After this, it really was a certainty that yet again, we would lose the penalty shoot-out – and we did, of course!

The European Championships in 2000 supplied more disappointment, but not quite at previous levels of hurt. We lost to Portugal 3-2 after being 2-0 up and if that wasn't enough, we then conceded an 89th minute penalty to give Rumania a 3-2 win against us and we were out again. In between, we even managed to beat Germany 1-0.

We had our Golden Generation in 2002 and actually a fine team. I watched that Brazil 2-1 quarter final loss at a hotel where I was attending a conference and again this didn't make it feel any better, being in a room with dozens of others. What sticks in my throat about this game was missing the chance to attack when they went down to ten men for the second half. We just laid down and died – oh dear, very un-English, but of course, we did have a pragmatic Swedish manager!

Next up it was 22nd June 2004 in Portugal and we were playing the hosts in the quarter finals of the European Championships. Leading 1-0 we conceded an equaliser seven minutes from time. It finished 2-2 and of course – we lost on penalties 6-5. I was all on my own in a hotel room, where were you? By now, I was sick of this pattern, weren't you?

However, there was more! The World Cup was held in Germany in 2006 and our son Tristan was now old enough to do his own thing and went over to watch the quarter final against Portugal. Now that mobile phones were more prevalent, he was able to share the whole experience with me; the singing around the town with the hordes of England fans, the sun drenched beer drinking, the tram trip to the ground and the worryingly long queue to get into the ground that meant that just got in at kick-off (I swear, I was as worried as him they might not get in). This extended to the regular post-match analysis and me telling Tristan from replays whether Beckham should have been sent off – he shouldn't!

That Ronaldo wink still riles me!

In 2008 we didn't qualify for the European Championship finals in Austria and Switzerland, but we still managed a traumatic and hurtful moment, going from winning, to losing and out, against Croatia at Wembley, defined forever by Steve McClaren and his hapless umbrella!

In South Africa we managed to draw with the USA and Algeria and a lucky win against Slovenia, before that shocking 4-1 thrashing by Germany. However, we managed to find an even more novel way to be disappointed as England fans, by Frank Lampard's equaliser that was a yard over the line, not being given. People often forget, but how different would that game have been if the goal was properly given? 2-0 down, coming back to 2-2 just before half time – in most cases you would say the team coming back from 2-0 down would be sure to win, but we had no VAR and we didn't!

It was a new kind of pain, wasn't it? Did this hurt you as much as any England defeat?

In Poland and Ukraine in the 2012 European Championships final, we played well in the group stages and then in the quarter final seem to just be completely outplayed by Italy, hang on to 0-0 through to penalties and then inevitably lose the penalty shoot-out. I personally found a new way to deal with this recurring hurt and in this tournament, that was in the USA, I was on business in the States when we played Italy.

In the USA, 'soccer' is not such a widespread big deal, so once we lost, I escaped all the soul searching that happens in England after such a disappointment. Also, I had the added bonus of the appalling performance and being so negative and outplayed – it seemed to dilute the pain, because by penalties I had NO expectations at all. Did you feel like this about this Italy loss?

In Brazil at the World Cup in 2014 we plummeted to new depths, not winning a game and finishing BOTTOM in a group TOPPED by Costa Rica! Would you believe it?

Well we needed to and it got worse! In the 2016 European Championships when we scrapped through to the quarter finals and were well beaten 2-1 by Iceland and all those great fans of theirs. Around this time, maybe in 2015, I stopped caring much about England games, it just hurt too much and after 50 years, I felt I had suffered one trauma too many!

I stopped being excited by the England football team, lost my passion and wondered whether it would ever return? I know I wasn't on my own, because Stuart of Ipswich stopped talking about England to me, Alan of West Ham stopped watching games, Tristan and I stopped analysing England games and nearly the whole country seemed to switch off from England internationals and focus on the club games.

However, nothing is forever and in the 2018 World Cup, England won me and most of the country back over. The ingredients were simple; a fresh, intelligent, ambitious, articulate and open young ENGLISH manager, a very young team playing with no fear and fast attacking football. It was magical and we were all onside again.

This tournament for me was exemplified by watching the first Paraguay game in a gastro pub over early dinner with my wife Marion (who hates football, but likes the fact that we were playing lots of bright, presentable and articulate young lads – nice young men), our daughter Natalie and her family, including two of our grandchildren. It was exhilarating to jump out of the chair so many times with my family, to celebrate a 6-0 win – unheard of! We even won a penalty shoot-out in the last 16. I know we lost to Croatia in the semi-final after extra time, but this felt different.

Is this hope false, or will the hurt finally stop soon? If 1966 is anything to go by, if we do win a tournament of note, I mean the European Championships or better still the World Cup, the country will celebrate like never before (well since 1966).

Fingers crossed.

Chapter 8

The Blood and Thunder
of the 1970s

Football in the 1970s was so very different to football today. I know this is stating the blindingly obvious, but as someone who experienced both and has had a powerful passion in each era, I think I am well positioned to reflect on what is different and what is the same and that's what I do in this chapter.

Let's start off the pitch and some of the differences, such as hooliganism, are obvious and covered in more detail in other chapters in this book. The first big difference was the effort needed to get to games. Road systems were appalling compared to today, although admittedly there are so many more cars on the road now-a-days. One of the reasons away support for mundane games was less than in modern times, was the sheer difficulty of getting to a game across the country. However, for big games they laid on coaches and those amazing British Rail Special Trains.

These train journeys were great days out and there was no ban on beer on these trains. Police rode on the trains and generally fans behaved well (perhaps not always). I loved away Special Trains, with a superb sense of excitement waiting on the station platform. I remember waiting on Winchester Railway Station platform at around 8.00 a.m. in the morning, waiting to board one of three Specials Trains to Liverpool for an FA Cup fifth round tie on 13th February 1971 and being so excited about the whole experience. In the ground at Anfield we were seated in a stand right by the Kop, who swayed backwards and forwards and moved half a dozen steps down when a goal was scored. It was magical, but dangerous. Away Day Specials are definitely a thing of the past and that's a shame.

Then, there was the food in the 1970s at grounds – well none, actually! In the grounds there was virtually nothing to eat and around the grounds, hamburger and hot dog vans were very limited. Eating out was not a common occurrence for working class families in the 1970s, although it did start to change as we entered the 1980s and we took this fresh air dining reticence with us to football games. When I go to most home games now-a-days, I meet-up with friend and colleague

Glenn at a local Noodle Bar and enjoy some excellent Asian Fusion food, whilst we watch the early game on his mobile smart phone and anticipate our team's match later. First one there buys the Tiger beers and orders the prawn crackers. The owners even know our standard order. How different is this to 1975 and a rushed two pints of Brown and Mild and a packet of crisps, with the salt in a blue wrapped bag in the crisp bag?

The watching experience, or more accurately 'not watching' experience in the 1960s and 1970s was very different to today. Of course, before Hillsborough and the Taylor Report we had very little seating – seating was for the posh people! I know a lot of people want to get back to some standing areas in grounds and I understand why they feel this way, as they want to get back to more dynamic atmospheres. However, I would like to point out a few imperfections from old school watching that were rife in the 1960s and 1970s. It was first come, first served, as you couldn't buy tickets in advance other than for big cup games or for seating. This meant that when you arrived late after work for midweek games you just about got in and spent the first 15 minutes of the match squeezing yourself down nearer the middle of the terrace. It wasn't a time to be a claustrophobic football fan!

Then, there was the issue of peeing (forget 'number twos', these were impossible). Once you got to the middle of the terrace, you weren't going anywhere. If you were lucky, you DIDN'T feel a warm and wet sensation on your calves, thanks to the big rough looking guy behind you, relieving himself into a rolled-up newspaper!

If you could make it to the urinals, they were absolutely disgusting – overflowing, smelly and no room to even shake. Worse than that, no usable hand basins – yuck!

Football fans were just as passionate in the 1970s as now and vice versa, however hooliganism was rife then and we will cover this in full in Chapter 9. Sometimes during the 1970s it was downright scary in the ground and now-a-days it tends to occur away from the ground and the police and clubs do seem to have got this mainly under control now. I love the passion and competitiveness of football and supporting YOUR CLUB, but for most ordinary law-abiding people, violence crosses a line. This doesn't apply to everyone, but then in society we have all sorts as well. If all standing areas means we go back to 1970s behaviours by fans, then I'm personally not in favour. The key factor might just be CCTV, which of course can monitor you, whether you are sat down or stood up!

There is another change from the 1970s to now and that is the profile of the people going to games and we cover this Prawn Sandwich Affect in detail in Chapter 14.

That's off the pitch comparisons, but what of on the pitch?

One big factor to consider when comparing the past to now, is the quality of the pitches. Today, in the Premier League, every pitch is immaculate with unscathed, bright green, flat and lined surfaces. These pitches are a mixture of real grass (97%) and artificial turf (3%), with amazing drainage systems and under-pitch heating. I avoided the term undersoil, because I'm not sure how much soil there is under that matting.

One home game against Leicester City, my team suffered a huge downfall of rain at 2.15 p.m. The whole pitch was covered in water and there seemed no way the game could go ahead. The rain stopped, they delayed the kick-off by 20 minutes, swept the water off the pitch to the side and the game was then played out on a perfect surface!

When my team enjoyed back to back promotions in 2010 and 2011, I like many thousands ran onto the pitch to celebrate. On both occasions, I was amazed by the extremely strong smell of fertilizer. Either that, or our team were going overboard with illegal substances – they weren't, it's a joke! Also, the mix of grass and artificial turf was only about half an inch thick, below it there was around four inches of soil, then hardcore. Let's compare this to the 1970s.

In the 1970s, most pitches started off OK in August, but as the winter progressed and games took their toll, the grass disappeared and was replaced by sand. Derby County's old Baseball Ground in the 1970s was the worst and yet Derby County won the 1st Division title (Premier League equivalent) on that dreadful pitch. When the ball hit the sand, it died, and bobbles were standard. Once we got to the end of season and Spring, the pitches dried up and became bouncing ball shows. It was like playing with a tennis ball on a road surface as kid. It was the same for both sides and players just accepted it as it was just the way it was!

Then, there were the footballs themselves. In the 1970s we had moved past those big heavy leather balls that when wet, were like cannon balls. This wasn't the case for me when playing for my local club, where heading the ball when saturated, required a serious amount of bravery, as it knocked your head back violently. However, in the top leagues, footballs were getting better, particularly after the Mexico 1970 World Cup. Despite this, in the 1970s, you virtually never saw the ball swerve or dip like you do today. It wasn't the players' lack of skills either, as there wasn't a more skilful player than George Best. Try and find a strongly swerving shot into the top corner from George in the 1970s, whereas now-a-days, even very ordinary players can bend it like Beckham!

On the field, the games really were rough and tumble. Referees let so much go without bookings or sending offs and this just encouraged tough tackling. The tackle from behind was fine and if you got the ball first, it didn't matter what you did. This encouraged some quite incredibly tough defenders and midfielders who became legendary. Norman Hunter of Leeds United was as tough a centre half as you could find, a total rock.

Ron 'Chopper' Harris didn't earn his nickname by gentle taps on the ankle and he was a rock like tough tackling full back for Chelsea for many years. He featured in one of the most feared defensive units of all time at Chelsea and with his scything tackling technique he left many a forward worse for wear on the ground. Dave Mackay was coming to the end of his career in the 1970s, but at Spurs and Derby County he was an intimidating defending who never ducked a challenge. Dave Mackay's confrontation with Billy Bremner is one of the more iconic football photographs in football history and it portrays how fiery the defender could be; mind you, Billy Bremner was no angel! Dave Mackay came back from several potentially career-ending injuries throughout his career, including a very bad broken leg and he really was an old school football warrior.

Nobby Stiles was a midfielder, but tackled like a defender and of course, won a World Cup winner's medal in 1966 and there were many more hard tackling and sometimes verging on 'dirty' players in football in the 1970s.

In this era, tough tackling and hard man play was considered a good thing and something to admire and the referees played their part. Goodness knows how skilful attackers even survived, let alone thrived and made a name for themselves. However, it was all we knew back then and it was exciting.

I have a suggestion for you; try watching 30 minutes of a standard 1st Division game from the early 1970s on YouTube and I promise you, that you will be astounded by the tackles that the players got away with.

If you shared this era with me, it's so much fun to reminisce, isn't it? However, if you didn't, believe me, it really was so very different to today.

It was genuinely blood and thunder, but it is was fun!

Chapter 9

Old School Hooliganism

The first thing I have to say is that hooliganism and bad behaviour is not limited to football fans and society has its fair share of people who don't value or respect the law, common decency and as a result, behave in an aggressive and confrontational way. However true this is, it needs to be acknowledged, that some football fans over the years have shown a side to them that is less than attractive!

It's no surprise really that football fans sometimes fall 'foul' of bad behaviours. The undiluted passion, the tribalism, the concentrated focus on winning and losing and not to be forgotten, plenty of alcohol flowing. It's no surprise really that hooliganism can sometimes rear its ugly head, especially with hormone-filled machismo young males.

In the 55 plus years I have followed and attended football matches, I have noticed several eras of hooliganism. This is not scientific and is based solely on my own reflections. The first era might be described as the 'Pure 1960s' and is the period where my memories are of football fans who were as passionate as now, but just a little more respectful of others and the law. Really, this reflects society generally then and now, but make no mistake, when beer flowed and someone said or did the wrong thing at the wrong time, fists would fly, even then.

Learning to lose with grace is something most hooligans don't do well and less than a year after my first game, my dad was taking me to another match, and this was against Wolves on a bright warm September Saturday in Division 2. He picked well again! My team's 9-3 win and to this date, it remains their biggest score. When we left the ground, we walked by a group of Wolves fans and as an excited and fanatical boy of eleven, I impulsively mocked them by saying, "What's the score Wolves?" My dad then pulled me to one side and gave me a serious dressing down.

He said, "Now listen, you never mock opposing fans, as they are very angry and not in the mood. Remember, they love their team like you do and how would you feel if we lost 9-3?" Then he led me back to the car and we didn't talk about it again. He was a wise man my dad, although to some today, in today's world of Social Media abuse and banter, perhaps this wisdom appears old fashioned.

The 1960s was a safer time for children to attend games. Other than when my brother or dad took me, I went to home games in the 1960s with just my friends. We would go to Saturday home games from where we lived in northern Hampshire and left home at about 9.00 a.m. and caught a bus to halfway, then changed bus, onto the city, although sometimes we were brave and extravagant enough to catch a train. We usually arrived in the city at around 11.30 a.m. and wandered over to the Top Rank, where we pretended to be hard and lulled around, until queuing outside the turnstiles waiting for them to open at 1.00 p.m. After the match, we reversed the trip and usually arrived home at about 7.30 p.m. It really was safe for 12 year olds to do this back then.

However, as the 1960s came to an end and we moved into the 1970s and I reached age 16, I noticed some significant changes and not just my own painful teenage hormonal changes!

The next era I refer to as the 'Angry 70s' and hooliganism went up a notch or two in this ridiculously crazy decade. My first personal experience of this was when I went to White Hart Lane on my own, to watch my team, not only lose heavily, but also get personally derided, humiliated and whacked by a bunch of Spurs fans and this was in the ground and during the game! Probably foolishly, for a lad of 16 on his own, I wore my team's scarf (designer kits didn't exist then), so you could say, "I deserved it". Whether I was wildly imprudent or not, it was a scary experience which was made additionally traumatic for me by being on my own. I felt very, very lonely in White Hart Lane that day and I have to say, resurfacing that memory is still painful.

The Angry 1970s hadn't started too well for me!

However, I wasn't to be solely on the receiving end of hooliganism and in 1973 I enjoyed a wild away trip, which I refer to as 'Y Viva Espana.'

You might be thinking, "What on earth does this refer to?" In fact, it is the title to a song that marked the beginning of Brits' love affair with the Mediterranean package holiday. However, it represents a key part in probably one of the best away days of my 'Football Supporting Career' and one that I look back on with a smile and as now, a mature granddad, a little shame.

It was early season and I was a boisterous 19-year-old who had just started training as a professional in an office. My friends and I, after several beers on Friday night, impulsively decided we had to go to Coventry the next day. It was a great decision, because Paggy, Pete and I had one of THOSE, away trips!

I should first ask any prudish readers to forgive me for my acts that day and remember I was only aged 19 at the time. For some of you though, my acts on this day might seem tame and it just shows perception is everything when it comes to this type of thing, but either way, it was fun. I will explain later in the chapter, the key part a song played in this day, but to start with it was a standard away day in 1973. Back then, my team didn't get a huge away following to mundane matches. Big games 'yes', but ordinary league games, we were only there in small groups.

We travelled up by car and parked in a multi-storey car park in town and then travelled to Highfield Road. As usual, my team lost, in a boring 2-0 match where we hardly had a shot at goal. To drown our sorrows, we retreated to a hostelry in Coventry and quite frankly, downed too many beers and too quickly!

We were 'in the zone' and getting more and more boisterous. Does this sound familiar? The pub had a jukebox and once we found the song Y Viva Espana, it then became even more rowdy. We played the song repeatedly and sang along to the words, "Viva Southampton." The song was written by Leo Roozenstraten and Leo Caerts and was originally performed by Samantha and released in 1971. You would know it if you heard it and it's a classic cheesy pop song of the 1970s.

It's been recorded in numerous languages and a hit in just about every country in the world. Sylvia Vrethammar's version spent six months in the UK chart, peaking at number four, but not with the words, "Viva Southampton!"

It starts with the poetic first line, "Oh this year we're off to sunny Spain – Y Viva Espana." This all sounds great fun doesn't it, but if you were a local sat in a Coventry bar and had four young lads from Hampshire taking over the whole pub with their beer induced singing antics, it probably ceased to have any charm at all. We were playing with fire!

However, along came our knights in shining armour. Two men in their twenties (looking very tough, I might add) came up to us and we expected the worse. They said to us, "Were you at the game today?" We answered "Yes" and then they said to us, "Now look lads, people are getting a little fed-up in here with your singing and THAT song, why don't we show you the Coventry nightlife and get you out of here, BEFORE you get into trouble?"

With that, they took us all around Coventry for a wild Saturday night, where they knew everyone and basically kept us out of trouble. When we bade them a fond farewell, we were a little inebriated!

However, without their protection (and it seemed people in Coventry respected them), it took us no time at all to get into trouble again. By the time we approached the multi-story car park, we were being chased by a group of yelling Coventry lads and stupidly we turned and charged them. Drink can make you do crazy things and this was one of those times. I have subsequently looked back at this event and realised how stupid and lucky we were when, despite outnumbering us, they turned and ran away from us. Bravado can work sometimes, but it was potentially a very dangerous choice.

The next two events are too embarrassing for me to fully record in this book (if I meet you in person, I will tell you the whole story), but the first involved two middle aged people in a dress suit and evening gown and the second involved me shaming myself in front of families at a motorway service station. Youthfulness can be boisterous, but in this instance, we escaped unharmed and had a wild away day to never forget.

Friend and business associate Alan told me of a trip to Upton Park that didn't go so well for an Everton away fan, who also behaved rather stupidly. Alan told me that opposite the renowned Pie and Mash shop (more on this later in Chapter 15) an Everton supporters' coach arrived for an evening game under floodlights. Apparently, one Everton supporter was the worse for wear and rather than keeping his head down, was according to Alan, "Giving it some!"

Unfortunately, his timing was all out, because at that moment, two of the West Ham Inter City Crew passed by. The rest is sadly all too predictable and Alan told me that the fellow was picked up and physically thrown through a shop front opposite the Pie and Mash shop (I assume, the Pie and Mash shop window would have been heresy to smash). Happily, Alan reported to me that remarkably the guy survived this assault and of course we do not condone violence in any form. However, it does go to prove that when drinking and away from home, it's important to be circumspect and sensible – or else unfortunately, stuff happens!

Another away game from the 1970s for me that could have gone very badly, was a trip to Manchester City, with I believe, the same protagonists that so nearly disgraced themselves at Coventry. It almost turned out to be a disaster, as well. There seems to be a recurring theme from the 1970s and my youth, of my friends and I making impulsive decisions to travel away when full of beers on a Friday night. I suspect some of you would recognise these situations yourself!

On Friday night in the pub, when happy and relaxed after a few beers, going to Maine Road the next day seemed like a great idea. Early

Saturday morning, perhaps less so! My friends and I were nothing if not diligent and at the agreed hour on Saturday morning we rose and met in the appointed meeting place to be picked up by one friend who was driving.

It was 7.30 a.m. which was very early after the night before and I remember the morning was extremely foggy. It was a moist and chilly October morning and if the truth be known, at 7.45 in the morning, we were all quietly regretting the previous night's decision to go to the Manchester City game. In fact, road conditions for the first two hours were downright dangerous. Another factor to consider is that in those days, young people like us, didn't own cars with all the mod coms of Sat Nav, air conditioning, seat warmers or high-tech media consoles. The best you could expect was a radio that worked on three stations and a car heating system that had 'On' and 'Off' as its settings!

On top of this, road systems in the UK in the 1970s were not as they are today, not by a long way. We had bits of motorways, but they didn't fully link up and as a result, journeys took longer. Now-a-days Hampshire to Manchester is probably three and a half hours to four hours on a good drive. Not in the 1970s it wasn't, probably more like five hours, plus! We also had a distinct lack of service stations and breakfast outlets, so planning stopping points became a big issue. These things matter when you are leaving home at 7.30 a.m. and arriving back home at about midnight. However, the fog did clear and it became a beautiful sunny autumnal October day. All was well, as we were on our way to watch our team and our hangovers were clearing.

We hadn't organised any tickets, no-one did then, so once we arrived in Manchester we decided to 'play safe.' Our 'play safe' idea was to buy seated tickets at Maine Road, which was City's ground then. Therefore, as soon as we arrived, we went to the ground to buy four tickets in the seated stand. So far, very sensible. We asked the girl in the ticket booth where she recommended, we sit and as it subsequently proved, she well and truly saw us coming.

She sold us four tickets together in the stand and we were happy. Off we went, back into Manchester to buy some food. After fish and chips and very good ones at that with curry sauce as a bonus, we were back on our way to the ground, wearing no colours and safe, unless we spoke and people heard our give-away Hampshire Hog accents!

If you went to Maine Road in the 1970s before it was knocked down, you will know it wasn't in the best of areas and around the ground it was generally a little intimidating for away fans, like us, all on their own. However, we were big lads and were quite well versed in football supporting and travelling. Well, at least we thought so!

When we got into our seats 30 minutes from kick off, it became increasingly obvious the girl in the ticket office had a warped sense of humour. We were right next to the City hard core fans, stood exactly to our right. I don't remember why, but in those days Maine Road had the whole of one huge stand as standing and their hard-core fans, stood right down one corner, in their thousands, right next to us!

Behind the goal was seating and we were sat here, close to the City boys. No problem though, we were safe and sat amongst lots of decent Manchester people who wouldn't harm a fly. Then my team had to go and spoil it all though! Mick Channon only went and scored and my team took the lead. Now, to give some perspective to what happened next; City were pretty good in the 1970s and in 1973, my team weren't! I sense you thinking, "What has changed?".

Therefore, when Mick scored, all four of us intuitively jumped up and celebrated hard. In an instant, we lost our anonymity and this wasn't helped by the very small number of away fans there that day. Suddenly, forty thousand eyes (well it felt like that many) were on us and glaring. Of course, then it started. Let me tell you, no matter how tough you feel, when several thousand people sing in tandem, with collective anger and frustration, directed at just four of you, "You are going to get your ****** heads kicked in" - it's worrying!

They meant it too and were very angry and pointing and looking straight at us. The collective group of hard core City fans quickly realised this was fun and that we were the Christians (well, we were Saints) to feed to the lions (them). Thus, the singing continued for some time and was personally directed at the four of us. Thankfully, they grew bored and joy of joys, City equalised and they forgot we existed. Did we really want City to score; "No, probably not", but we weren't too upset either?

Did you ever not 'wish for', but equally, weren't too upset when the other side scored? For your sake, I hope not.

We escaped the stadium intact and no hordes were outside to meet us when we left the ground (they knew what we looked like). We lived to fight another day and Maine Road in October 1973 was my Dunkirk.

One other game from that era, that did involve fisticuffs and the most planned hooliganism I ever saw, was surprise, surprise against Millwall at the Dell. It was 18th April 1975 and we took our usual spot under the stand. There was a relatively small crowd in, as the season was already going nowhere. Then at 2.50 p.m. exactly, I witnessed the most co-ordinated hooliganism I had ever seen, or in fact experienced since.

At 2.50 p.m. exactly, someone blew a referee's whistle very loudly and with that three fellas to our left started randomly violently punching those around them. They were Millwall fans without any colours and acting on the order from the whistle. Literally, all around the ground, in little pockets, a similar thing was happening and suddenly there was absolute mayhem. As you can imagine, they were quickly overwhelmed by weight of numbers and the police's intervention.

However, while it lasted, it was crazy. Looking back now, the most amazing thing about this 1970's classic hooliganism was the unadulterated planned and managed nature of this 'event.' Quite frankly and in a strange way, it was impressive, but hard to understand.

My personal experiences of Millwall hooliganism was not unique to me and during the 1970s, Millwall's tight band of hooligans became notorious. They were known as the 'Millwall Bushwackers' and some of their acts were legendary amongst football fans at the time.

This wasn't helped by a BBC TV Panorama documentary, which rather than dispelling the hooligan myth, blew it out of proportion and caused an uproar. The show proved to be very damaging for Millwall FC itself but did build still further the legend of the 'Miillwall Bushwackers'. On 11th March 1978 a riot broke out at the Den during a FA Cup quarter-final between Millwall and Ipswich, with friend and colleague Stuart's Ipswich team winning 6-1 away. Fighting began on the terraces and spilled onto the pitch with dozens of fans injured, with some hooligans turning on their own team's supporters. It was carnage and the legendary Ipswich manager, the late Sir Bobby Robson said, "They should have turned the flamethrowers on them!" A little dramatic, I think, Sir Bobby, but we understand what you were trying to say!

Ipswich Stuart also told me of an occasion when his brush with hard core hooliganism was extremely unsettling and I think an eye opener to all of us. Apparently, he and a friend decided to go to a Boxing Day Ipswich match away at Fulham. He left his friend to organise tickets and coach travel. So far, so good.

However, once on the coach at Ipswich it became apparent that Stuart and his friend were on a coach with the hard core Ipswich Crew, 'The Ipswich Punishment Squad'. Stuart told me that it was very uncomfortable all trip with his compatriots constantly angry and looking for trouble. Stuart and his friend even contemplated getting the train home after the match to avoid this environment. Their fellow travellers even stole the match ball and enticed the police to the coach after the game. Stuart told me that he and his friend were very relieved to escape from the coach later that night and go to a normal pub and enjoy a quiet pint away from the angry madness. Doesn't this just say everything about the difference between the small hooligan minority and ordinary decent people who just love their team?

On a similar note, friend and business associate Alan told me of his trip to the West Ham versus Middlesbrough FA Cup semi-final on 23rd April 2006 at Villa Park. The traffic police sent Alan's car full of his children and him to park right in the middle of all the Middlesbrough coaches and Alan told me just how intimidating the long walk to the ground turned out to be, with a few drunk Boro fans bullying and cajoling the five of them all the way to Villa Park. When you are the receiving end, this sort of thing can be very unsettling.

In 1976, my team achieved their greatest moment when they won the FA Cup beating Manchester United and needless to say, the Angry 1970s didn't let me down with a good sprinkling of hooliganism experiences in that cup run, which I will share with you.

At the 5th Round tie away at West Brom the game was not all ticket and West Brom were completely thrown by so many away fans unexpectedly attending. Estimates are that there were between 10,000 and 15,000 away fans in the crowd of 36,634. The stand behind the goal was all standing back then. One of my main memories of this game is holding a Riot Policeman's helmet for five minutes in my hand. There were some West Brom fans in the stand with the thousands of my team's fans and when West Brom scored, not unexpectedly, it all kicked off behind the goal. Back in the 1970s, Riot Police were never far away at games and they waded in with some relish when the trouble erupted.

As they took a troublemaker past me to eject him from the ground, the Riot Policeman's shield fell on the ground and as he bent down to pick it up, his helmet fell into my hands. Some five minutes later he came back for it and I'm glad I didn't do anything with his helmet whilst he was away, as he had a huge truncheon!

I had some family commitments on 6th March 1976 when my team travelled to Valley Parade to play Bradford City in the 6th Round and decided I just couldn't make it. My friends who did go, paid the price for us taking the lead and for the rest of the game and all the way back to the station were relentlessly attacked by home fans. One friend came back with a black eye and cuts and another luckily avoided serious injury, when a five-litre beer keg was thrown at my team's fans from above them and just missed his head.

Onto the semi-final and the violence continued!

My team's fans were given the Shed End at Stamford Bridge, which was a major coup when it came to support that day and 21,500 of my team's fans were in the ground. However, it didn't start well as the first thing that happened when we arrived, was all our coach party were ambushed down a side street by 150 odd Chelsea Crew hooligans, all without colours. I guess they didn't like the Shed being red and white that day. It was a full blooded brawl, although thankfully no weapons were used and many in our group entered the ground that day with cuts and bruises. However nasty this was, we survived, and nothing was ruining this day for us, which incidentally my team won, which unless you are a Crystal Palace fan (that's who my team played), you wouldn't remember it!

The final was held on 1st May 1976, which was a bright beautiful day. Our coach driver parked us up our team's part of the Wembley car park and we relaxed and went walk-a-bout. In 1976, hooliganism was rife and almost at its peak and at the Manchester United versus Derby County semi-final there was a mass pitch invasion and brawl. This was serious hooliganism and trouble was anticipated at Wembley, because Manchester United were seen as the worst behaved supporters (well, maybe after Millwall).

Almost immediately we left the coach in the Wembley car park, I was approached by some rough looking United fans and one said to me,

"Give us your ticket or I will use this!" He had an object sticking out under his coat, that looked like a knife. Sometimes in life you have those big moments where what you decide there and then, impacts directly on how things turn out for years to come and this was one such moment!

I replied to him, "Now look mate, I have waited years for this and I don't expect it will ever happen again, so if you want my ticket, you need to do better than that." Bizarrely, he said, "Fair enough", shrugged his shoulders and walked off with his friends. I have looked back on this moment and shuddered to think of how it could have turned out and so much so, that I might not be writing this book now. Equally, it was probably a fake knife and I probably called his bluff. Either way, I know I had a dry mouth, but I also had my TICKET!

Onto what I call the 'One Step Too Far 1980s' era of hooliganism. The worst trouble at games didn't end after the 1970s and in 1985, possibly the turning point in bad behaviour was reached with the Kenilworth Riot. This occurred at the FA Cup 6th round game at Luton's Kenilworth Road on 13th March 1985 where Luton beat Millwall 1-0. There were numerous pitch invasions, fighting in the stands and missile-throwing with one object hitting Luton's goalkeeper Les Sealey. Prior to the game, Luton were allegedly asked by Millwall to make the Wednesday night match all-ticket, but this was supposedly ignored. As a result, rival hooligan firms also reportedly gained access to the ground. As well as the Millwall hooligans and those belonging to Luton, many of the paltry 31 fans arrested after the violence were identified as being from Chelsea's Headhunters and West Ham's Inter City Firm. The riot was widely covered on TV and outraged society and was in fact, the beginning of the end of hard core unchecked hooliganism. The FA commissioned an inquiry and more importantly Maggie Thatcher declared war on football hooliganism.

Friend and associate Newcastle John, told me of a tale many years ago of a Newcastle United match at home to West Ham United where the terrace behind the goal was separated by high temporary fencing into;

home fans section, 'no go' section, away fans, another 'no go' section and then home fans. Apparently, every 5 to 10 minutes, a crazy Geordie would run head first and scale the fence, run across the 'no go' area, dodging police to then repeat their athleticism, by jumping head first into the Cockney Hordes, where after a few flaying fists they would be set upon, before being overcome by the Londoners and then rescued by the police before they got seriously hurt.

Why - who knows? Probably, because they saw that they were being invaded by a tribe from the South or more likely, just because they could!

He also told me of a crazy European Fairs Cup semi-final match with Glasgow Rangers, where 15,000 Scottish fans descended on Newcastle and riots exploded all the way back to the railway station and as a young child, he remembers police on large horses and much shouting and yelling.

Back in the 1970s and early 1980s, the walk back to the car or station after a match always involved some fisticuffs occurring around you. It was common practice and although still does occur to this day, is very much the exception rather than the rule.

This did continue into the 1990s, but as all-seater stadiums came into top league football, clubs and police were able to get better control over hooliganism in the grounds, with much of the fighting taking place now away from the grounds. Films like Green Street in 2005 seemed to threaten to rebirth and glamorise hooliganism and as far as I can see, to this day it simmers under the surface, waiting to reignite.

If you have attended football games for any length of time, you must have seen your own share of football violence. Of course, you might even be a member of a 'crew'. Do you agree that with the trouble now mainly occurring away from the ground and 'crews' tending to fight each other, rather than innocent people, things have improved for the vast majority of non-violent fans?

The one episode I remember the most was of course that incredibly carefully orchestrated act by the Millwall Bushwackers at the Dell on 18th April 1975, which was cold-blooded madness, but strangely impressive in its planning.

At least at Maine Road in October 1973, we were told what they were going to do to us and specifically our heads, but at the Dell in April 1975, we didn't get any warning at all - apart from a whistle

Chapter 10

Programmes and Stickers

Football has always drawn obsessive collectors to it and this began with cigarette cards, well before any of us was born. It all started in the USA in the nineteenth century when Wills produced their first set of cigarette cards, 'Ships and Sailors', followed by 'Cricketers' in 1896. In 1906, Ogden's produced a set of Association Football cards depicting footballers in their club colours, in one of the first full-colour sets of cards.

The door to obsessive collecting had opened for football fans, particularly young impressionable fans.

I know today, football cigarette cards attached to sport doesn't necessarily feel correct due to health issues and in fact, this all changed in 1978 when Panini launched their World Cup stickers. For children of two generations, this Italian company and others, were to provide so much collective pleasure.

Our son Tristan started his serious schoolboy collecting at the 1990 Italian World Cup with the Panini Italia Stickers. He told me that at aged 9 he could be found moving around the school playground to hustle and exchange prime stickers. He wasn't on his own and this has been repeated at major football championships ever since. Once Tristan reached full teenager status, it clearly wasn't acceptable to be seen to be a sticker collector – it just wasn't cool.

However, the good news for all of us, is that once you grow up and have your own children, you can revisit collecting with them and it's OK, all over again. There is always one card that's almost impossible to get, isn't there – like Willie Wonker's Golden Ticket? Do you think the companies deliberately only print a small number of these elusive cards, to add to the anticipation? I think they do! It's a form of addiction, you know.

Do you still have any of your old childhood collections in your loft or in a cupboard hidden away? Now-a-days it's not just at big tournaments that stickers reign supreme, as now we have Premier

League Match Attax cards, so just as in football generally, the commercial opportunities are maximised by those clever marketeers.

Programme collecting has been around the whole time I have been a football fan and isn't there something special about the smell of a freshly printed programme, straight out of the box? You could read it briefly at the ground, but then read in detail when home and importantly, have a memento of the match you attended.

I had a tremendous programme collection when I was a schoolboy.

I held an England schoolboy international programme from 1964 with several future stars playing as under 16s, as well as a few FA Cup finals, England internationals and of course my own team's games. Paul the Greek beat me though, to this day he has 40 years' worth of Manchester City programmes and for every single game he attended. Now that's impressive!

Paul has also kept a scrapbook of every Manchester City game he has watched in person over his 40 years of support. I bitterly regret throwing away my childhood scrapbooks, so well done Paul.

Now-a-days these old collections are worth quite a lot of money. The current world record for a single-sheet programme is for the 1909 FA Cup final between Manchester United and Bristol City which went for £23,500 in 2012.

In the same year, a family from Ipswich managed to collect approximately £46,000 by auctioning off a set of football programmes they stumbled across in their house - check your loft Stuart!

With the onset of digital media, hard copy programme sales are dramatically falling although you can order them from most clubs, AFTER the game, so the clubs can print to order and not be stuck with thousands of unsold programmes. This is a shame, as programmes sellers around the ground, yelling, "Programme" at the top of their voice, is a happy memory for me and probably yourself.

In fact, programme selling was a family business for us Walters. Our son Tristan helped fund his extensive university alcoholic beverages by selling programmes one week at Chelsea and one week at Fulham, when he was at university in London. He told me how it was very quiet for the first hour and then 45 minutes from kick-off it went crazy.

He still growls when recalling how one chap, every week, would throw a fake Scottish £20 note at him, just when it was at its most hectic and Tristan would give him his change. If it was you who did this every match and you are reading this now – shame on you, as it came out of Tristan's pocket.

He also told me that he saw lots of 'Love' 'Hate' tattooed letters as people handed their cash over. Tristan 'hated' standing in the cold every week, but 'loved' getting to see the second half of games for free after cashing up!

We still have programmes at grounds now (just) and at every big tournament, to this day, schoolchildren can be seen actively swapping cards in the playground, so the love for football stickers and programmes continues.

Viva those collectables!

Chapter 11

Those Rare Geniuses and Classic Entertainers

It really hurts when your team loses, doesn't it? We know our team can't win every game, but reality can be a bitter pill to swallow. This brings us to those very rare football geniuses and classic entertainers and I suffered at the feet of such a genius in his prime.

It was 27th November 1971 and despite my natural disappointment, that day all my team's fans had to simply accept that a pure football genius must be acknowledged and applauded. It was a dark and wet Saturday afternoon and the recent European Champions, Manchester United were in town. Despite this, my hopes were high.

The ground was packed to the rafters with over 30,000 in and my excitement was added to when my dad's friend collapsed with the crush and had to be carried out before the game started. Don't worry, we picked him up from the First Aid Centre - but after the game, of course!

Not only did my dad's friend collapse, but so did my team. The problem was, that this Manchester United team included Bobby Charlton, Brian Kidd, Alex Stepney, Sammy Mcllroy and the genius that was George Best. My team tried hard and ran about a lot, but George Best literally took them apart and scored a magnificent hat trick, with the third goal being a classic dribbling masterpiece. It was the work of a pure genius and I think it's the only time I saw my team's fans applaud an opponent - he was that good.

Watching George Best waltz around my team's defence at will, was a salutary lesson in humility.

I never saw Messi in the flesh and only watched Ronaldo when he was young at Manchester United. Legends and geniuses are titles too easily spread around, so I will simply reference a few of the rare talents I have seen live (not on TV, as you can't appreciate their talent on screen). in my 55 plus years of football supporting.

Jimmy Greaves was the best goal poacher I watched, but also an amazing dribbler. Gary Lineker was a great goal scorer and I will never forget that hat trick in the 1986 World Cup against Poland, which was a jump out of the chair time (I think around 11.00 p.m. UK time) and without it, we wouldn't have had that 'Hand of God' experience – thanks Gary!

Thierry Henri was the best all round attacker I saw, with the ability to destroy you and he did many times, including once against Ireland with his hand! Alan Shearer was probably the one centre forward, as a defender, you wouldn't want to play against, and I saw him play for my team when he was starting his career as an 18 to 21 year old. He was one of the last truly great old school centre forwards.

Ryan Giggs was a superb player over many years for Manchester United and his FA Cup goal against Arsenal after an exciting dribble and shot was another of those, "Not my team, but jump out of the chair moments". Kevin Keegan was another consistently superb player who thrived at whatever club he went to; Liverpool, Hamburg, Southampton and Newcastle – oh, and Scunthorpe!

Bobby Charlton was a great all round player who could, shoot, dribble, head and pass and won the World Cup with England and of course, he always behaved impeccably. I have to mention Matt Le Tissier and although not achieving the heights with medals and caps, other than George Best, the most exciting and unpredictable player I watched on a football pitch. Look on You Tube at his 30 best goals - he just didn't score ordinary goals (especially against Newcastle United).

Friend and business associate John of Newcastle United supporting fame told me he can't bear to hear Matt Le Tissier's name, as it conjures up his Post Traumatic Stress Disorder (PTSD) with the memories of all those Le Tiss goals against his team and I understand why!

David Beckham and Graeme Souness were fine players and Souness was as tough a midfielder as I ever saw. He was so competitive and determined. Kenny Dalglish was annoyingly superb.

However, two of my favourite players over the last 55 years were Bobby Moore and Gordon Banks, both sadly no longer with us. Both were perfect gentlemen and simply magnificent in their positions. Over the last 55 years, England hasn't had that many truly world class great players and these two were the best in the world in their positions, for many years and by some distance. I was privileged to have watched them both play at their peak.

Every club has a history, with games of the century, best seasons ever, legendary players and something I feel is really cute – sacrosanct shirt numbers. These are numbers worn by historic club legends over the years and seen by the fan base as holy shirt numbers and without doubt, a grave responsibility for the current incumbents.

My club's holy number is Number 7, whose past players included Terry Paine (over 700 appearances and played one game in England 1966 World Cup), Kevin Keegan (whilst reigning European Player of the Year), Matt le Tissier (Le God) and Sir Rickie Lambert (SRL).

The Newcastle United Number 9 shirt is memorable and has been worn by Jackie Milburn, Wyn Davies, Super Malcom McDonald, Les Ferdinand and of course Alan Shearer. West Ham have retired the Number 6 shirt in honour of the late, great Bobby Moore. I'm sure your club has its own sacrosanct shirt number and no doubt you are remembering your great players from the past, right now.

The Digital Age has many advantages, especially for us authors. However, predictive spell-check is a mischievous devil and if our edit team have missed a 'Booby Moore' (why does it do this, as Bobby is a word), then I apologise to this great man and his memory!

My personal highlight over these 55 years was no doubt about it, that of seeing the genius that was George Best in his pomp and in person. Law, Best and Charlton and even though my team lost 5-2 at home...wow!

It was an, "I was there moment"

Chapter 12

Is Your Club a Big Club?

I have heard it said that size doesn't matter, particularly when women are being gracious to their menfolk. However, we all know this is not completely true and in some areas of life, not just intimacy, size does have an effect.

Perhaps this explains British football fans' obsession with 'BIG'. On the talk radio stations, you will hear endless debates on whether Club X is a BIG CLUB and ex-players, who now hold themselves out as journalists, are the worse. This is probably because it seems that all the radio channels and TV channels only employ ex-players of, here we go – BIG CLUBS!

Presently, (and it is only at the moment) the BIG SIX (there, I'm doing it too) are indisputably; Manchester City, Liverpool, Spurs, Chelsea, Arsenal and Manchester United. See below, shot from typical BIG SIX Premier League match – I jest, of course, and it's grass roots, pub football, but it's still football, isn't it?

Of course, things change, but some recently released statistics show the average standings in the leagues over the last 50 years (just about most of my supporting career) and it really isn't very surprising.

Sometimes statistics can confuse, but in this case, the following statistics can't be argued with and here is the REAL 'Big Club' league table over 50 years:

1. Liverpool.
2. Arsenal.
3. Manchester United.
4. Spurs.
5. Everton.
6. Chelsea.
7. Manchester City.
8. Aston Villa.
9. Newcastle United.
10. West Ham United.
11. Southampton.
12. Leeds United.
13. Ipswich Town.
14. Leicester City.
15. Norwich City.
16. Middlesbrough.
17. Nottingham Forest.
18. Derby County.
19. West Brom.
20. Sunderland.

Thirteen of these twenty have actually won the league and seven have not. Eleven have won European competitions and nine have not.

Therefore, what is a big club? Is it past achievements, is it history, is it size of crowds, is it potential i.e. catchment area? What is it?

In reality, it seems to be what suits the person arguing the point. How on earth can anyone argue that Leeds United is not a big club, but it's currently miles away from the top six teams and their vast monetary wealth and they are 12th in the overall league placings over 50 years? Why do we have such a hang-up on whether we are big or not? I loved my time with my club in League One and reconnecting with grass roots football. I have enormous respect for fans of lower league clubs who turn up, week in and week out to support the team they love. I know the Top Six teams have just as passionate fans, but they also attract what we non-Top Six teams' fans call 'Plastics'.

These are people who jump on the band wagon because they need a Designer Team. I can't imagine Leyton Orient (a club I have great affection for, as a result of a number of memorable away days at Brisbane Road) having ANY plastic fans!

Outside the Top Six, one million people regularly watch their team's home games. Think about that, it's an incredible number of not just passionate fans, but people who pay to go along, rain and shine. In fact, three times more people watch non-top Six Teams play live, as watch Top Six teams! However, include the people who follow, but don't watch, those who watch on TV in the Far East and buy designer replica shirts and the ratio reverses!

As I previously stated, I loved being in League One and it felt strange being a BIG CLUB at this level – I'm not used to this!

How do Manchester City fans handle being 'Top Dog' after so many earlier humbling experiences? My answer would be, so far quite well. They still retain their dignity and some humility, but how long will that last, as older fans with long memories die off and the new keyboard generation come on the scene? Paul the Greek is just such an example of this long standing City fan humility. It's hard to believe today in times of such Manchester City triumph, but Paul supported them for 34 years before City actually won a trophy.

I can remember watching live that 1999 Manchester City versus Gillingham League Two play-off final when Gillingham went 2-0 up with an 87 minute goal and City then scored two goals in injury time, with the equaliser being the last kick of the game, to then win on penalties and start their move back to glory. Paul was there of course and recalls how he nearly broke his ankle going mad when the equalizer went in. He was also there 10 yards from the celebrations when Sergio Aguero scored the most famous Premier League goal ever against QPR to win the league with the last kick of the season. Despite this glorious moment, Paul still reflects that the Gillingham moment was bigger for him, as it represented a turning point in City's fortunes. Such moments turn on a dime and it was only two decades ago.

The UK TV series, 'Whatever Happened to the Likely Lads?' was first shown in the 1970s. If you haven't watched it, the series featured two working class Geordie lads (Newcastle fans) living through a time of great change with one moving from his Working Class roots into the new Middle Class.

In my opinion, it's a classic comedy series and in one particular episode, first shown in 1974, as a result of a bet, the boys have to spend all day avoiding the score of the Bulgaria versus England game, which is played in the afternoon and on TV in the evening.

They while away some of the time in their local pub, talking about life generally. Terry discloses to Bob he doesn't like Koreans and this expands into his dislike of the whole of Asia, Russians, Egyptians, Italians, French, Spanish, Danes and Americans! He has a crude generalisation about each and every nations' peoples, which I can't repeat in this 'politically correct' book! He finishes by saying that he doesn't much like the Welsh, Scots or Irish and then reflects he doesn't like Southerners, nor people from Sunderland and in fact doesn't much like the people down his road and isn't a great fan of his neighbours!

It's very funny and mocks these types of sweeping unintelligent generalisations. Why not have a look at the scene on the scene on YouTube and see what you think?

I believe we must not take this approach with our fellow football team fans and maybe all fans should have more humility and genuine respect for other passionate supporters. Big Club or Small Club, they aren't our foes (other than twice a season when we play them), they are our passionate football fan, brothers and sisters.

Chapter 13

Those Gut Wrenching Moments

We all have them, even the BIG CLUBS' fans! I am referring to those moments and games, or even seasons, that cut right to your emotional bone.

These are the events that you don't forget and stay with you for the lifetime of your support. With fellow supporters of your club, there is a collective trauma that generally gets easier as time elapses and also future positive memories replace these old traumas, but you never forget!

It's not surprising that with so much passion involved and love of your club and the fact that football is unpredictable and hyper-competitive, such disappointments occur. In this chapter I reflect on some gut wrenching moments, some on the pitch and some off it.

I will start this 'quasi group counselling session' by me sharing a wound that goes back many years and in fact doesn't include actually watching a game of football. As a teenager coming up to age 16, this was a time when I couldn't get enough of my team. However, as no doubt you can equate to, it doesn't always go as you planned. Sometimes my dad would take me to games and sometimes my friends would join me. Occasionally I was so passionate about seeing a game that no-one else wanted to see, that I went unaccompanied. Unfortunately, such was my passion, I sometimes did impulsive things. One such occasion was in 1970 when my team were away at West Bromwich Albion, in February.

I pig-headedly decided I was going on my own, even though I was only 16 and despite the protestations of my parents. Back then, kids grew up quicker than they do now-a-days and many lads were out working with grown men in factories at aged 16, so it wasn't quite as rash as it might appear today. I had little money and no transport, so I walked to the A34 and hitch-hiked. It was a bitterly cold day and I waited for an hour, as cars and lorries whisked by, but eventually a kind man picked me up. We drove on to Birmingham in his warm car and we chatted about football (he was a Sheffield Wednesday fan). As we neared Solihull, the car radio announced that the West Brom v Southampton game was postponed due to a frozen pitch.

I was devastated, all that effort to get there on my own and now no match to watch. He kindly dropped me at Birmingham New Street railway station, bid me farewell and I caught a slow train home with several changes and arrived home cold, bedraggled and forlorn at 7.00 p.m. I don't think my dad actually said, "I told you so", but really, he had every right to say it to me. However, the frustration and disappointment and failure of this day in 1970 where I put so much personal effort into, has lived with me for 50 years. Did you ever suffer this way, desperately trying to get to a game, maybe car breaking down, missing a flight, or similar? It's an awful memory, isn't it, feeling so out of control?

Son in law Jon of Norwich City fan fame told me that he had a similar experience when going on a Norwich City fans' coach to the old Highbury and an Arsenal versus Norwich game. He told me that when they left East Anglia there was no bad weather around and the fans were in good spirits. Apparently, as they joined the M25, the coach driver announced that there was fog at Highbury, although the match looked fine to go ahead. Thirty minutes from Highbury, he announced it was no worse. You know what's coming next! Five minutes from Highbury and less than an hour to kick-off, they were told to turn around and go back to Norfolk – match postponed!

Paul the Manchester City fan recalls travelling all the way to Plymouth for a Tuesday night game in League One and when they got past Exeter, they heard on the radio the match was postponed due to a waterlogged pitch. Needless-to-say, it rained all the way down and all the way back and was demoralising. You see, even Big Six fans suffer, although back then Manchester City were far from a Big Six team. We have all been here, haven't we? Imagine the mood on that Norwich coach or the car turning around at Exeter. It's worse than losing, isn't it?

Friend and colleague Stuart told me that his biggest heartache as an Ipswich Town fan was a visit to Old Trafford on 4th March 1995. He told me that he had 'Man Flu' at the time, so only went because his friend didn't want to go on his own. What a bad decision Stuart!

Ipswich lost 9-0 and to make matters worse, Stuart told me that his seat at Old Trafford was broken and he had to sit atop it, all game. He told me that his abiding memory of this tragic day was hearing the United fans singing, "We want 10" and the Ipswich fans instantly replying with the memorable chant (given the circumstances) of, "We want one" You have to love this instant football fan black humour, don't you?

Even though they lost 9-0, Manchester United were very good then and Stuart tells me that he feels that when his team lost 7-0 at Peterborough, it felt worse!

Old Trafford appears a particularly challenging venue for my friends and fans of other clubs, because West Ham Alan remembers his trip on April Fool's Day 2000. Apparently, West Ham foolishly took the lead and then preceded to concede seven goals in a humiliating 7-1 defeat.

I think perhaps my biggest heartbreak (before 2019) as a fan of my team goes back to 17th March 1979, which was a cold, snowy day with unseasonably low temperatures and the 1978 League Cup Final at the old Wembley with my team playing Nottingham Forrest. There was even talk that the game might not go ahead and if you watch carefully on old YouTube videos, you will see snow that was swept off the Wembley pitch, stacked up around the side-lines. It was another great Wembley occasion with a crowd of 96,952 (I'm still short of being in a 100,000 crowd).

With the passing of time, I have forgotten just what an achievement it would have been to have beaten Nottingham Forest that day. This was a great football team with a great manager and I use the description 'great' with due consideration. They won the First Division in the season after promotion in 1978 and finished second in the league in the 1978-79 season. Only 17 weeks after the cup final against my team, they WON the European Cup (today's Champion League) by beating Malmö FF 1-0 with a goal from Trevor Francis, England's first million-pound player. They also retained the European Cup the next season.

They were a superb team.

It was cold, snowy and my team were facing Cloughie and his great side. My late brother went with me to the game after returning permanently from Australia with his family and we drove up in his car and parked in the Wembley car park. We purchased tickets from someone who knew someone and these were neutral tickets on the halfway line. Of course, I would have preferred to be behind the goal with my team's fans, but we were at least there.

In the first half, my team were excellent and deservedly led 1-0. The second half was somewhat different and Forest came charging out.

Gary Birtles equalised after 51 minutes, as a direct result of a bad mistake and hesitation by Chris Nicholl. It was like the Alamo after that and my team held out until 11 minutes from time, when Birtles and Woodcock scored, before Nick Holmes scored a great consolation goal.

We were very depressed that day, because it really was the proverbial game of two halves and they are particularly hard to take when your team's half was the first. I don't know when your worst game was, but 40 plus years later, I can still recall the stomach churning feeling when the second goal went in; please beware, these feelings can hang around! Sorry if I reminded you of your own traumatic memory.

I wasn't the only one feeling frustrated, as outside in the Wembley car park it was absolute carnage, even by 1970s standards. I witnessed some of the worst fighting I have seen at a game, well certainly at a big game and at Wembley. It was both sets of fans involved and instigating the violence and people were going onto the other sides' coaches and huge punch-ups erupted. It wasn't pretty at all and although I was already depressed, this made things feel even worse. However, irrespective of the disappointment, at least I could say, "I was there."

40 years later it was to get worse!

As we have established, supporting a football club is full of passion, pleasure and it has to be said – PAIN. I'm afraid my own worst moment of pain supporting my team will stay with me and fellow fans of my team, forever. It was of course, my team's home loss to Leicester City on 25th October 2019. This game was a genuine nightmare, almost literally from start to finish. The tragedy is that virtually every single one of you reading this, will know the score of the match and that's humiliating for me and the fans of my team!

For the sake of completeness, the score was 0-9 and that's not a typographical error.

At the time of writing, it equalled the record score (nine) in the Premier League era, it was the largest ever home defeat in the top-flight division in the 131 years since the Football League was formed and my own team's record loss and needless-to-say, highest home loss.

That's VERY, VERY bad, isn't it?

We had a man sent off after 12 minutes but really this wasn't the main reason for the size of the loss, it was the capitulation by the players on the field, just like a schoolboy game. I remember I played in a schoolboy game for my youth club against our bitter local rivals in front of a crowd of at least 250 people (it was usually 5 or 6 watching). We held them for 20 minutes and then the floodgates opened and we lost 10-0.

But … we were only 15 years old, not very good, playing away from home and we were not paid millions of pounds salary a year to play football!

As you can see, I'm still very angry about this Leicester City humiliation.

That Friday night of 25th October 2019 was made additionally traumatic because the game was live on Sky TV and of course, it poured with rain, driven by strong winds all game. I looked at the weather forecast before I left home and it said, "Maybe a light shower at 9.00.p.m.". Therefore, I went to the match just in a T-shirt and jumper. When I arrived home at 11.00 p.m. that night after the match, dripping wet, bedraggled and emotionally battered, even my football hating wife Marion, took pity on me.

By half-time (0-5), around half of the crowd of 30,000 plus had left in disgust. I nearly did, but those around me persuaded me to stay and I'm really glad they did. Those that stayed, the hard core, went into a form of heroic defiance and sang all of my team's songs for virtually the whole of the second half, including many songs about players from the past. It was heart-warming defiance and I suspect would and has happened with any fans around the country in a similar hopeless situation. That hard core of a club's fans really loves their team, irrespective of circumstances. However, despite this surprising slant, it was the worse time as a fan I EVER experienced over 55 plus years of support and I certainly hope I never again have to go through anything remotely similar. Since writing this, it is possible my team have lost by even more than 9-0, but please; no!

I was at a family event the day after this humiliating loss and it was a strange experience to be a form of 'celebrity for a day', with everyone wanting to find out, "How I felt". I even received texts from people around the country that I hardly knew, commiserating with me, such was their empathy with my fan's pain. It felt a little like people were rubber-necking me, similar to what you see on the opposite side of a motorway after a road accident. That wet, wild, Autumnal evening accurately represents the extreme PAIN of being a passionate fan of your team.

As an aside, if you are a Sunderland fan and a few years ago had to live through my team's demolition of you 8-0, then I am genuinely sorry. With the benefit of hindsight, I wish we had only won 5-0 against you and saved you all, your own humiliation. Let me ask you now, "Do you ever get over this type of trauma?"

Please, please – tell me you do!

Paul the Greek's lowest Manchester City moment was away at Lincoln in League One on a Wednesday night. Paul took three days off work and stayed with an old friend to then suffer a 4-1 hiding that Paul says could have been 10-1! Of course, inevitably it rained as well on a Wednesday night away trip in Lincoln. Does this sort of experience sound familiar (maybe not 9-0) and of course, that's the pain I being a fan?

We all suffer these moments and they are not necessarily the moments you would expect that hurt the most. It's clear that football can be harsh to we passionate fans and to every story, there are two sides; Manchester United's two injury time goals in the 1999 European Cup Final to Bayern Munich's fans despair at throwing away a lead in injury time. Next time you suffer one of these traumatic events when supporting your team, why not remind yourself that you have to suffer the lows, to enjoy the highs?

You just don't ever know which side you will be on or when it will happen, but that's why we love it!

Chapter 14

Away Day Jaunts

There really is something about a good away day, isn't there?

We have all enjoyed them and often it doesn't matter who wins or loses, as it's the experience that counts. More than anything else, this chapter exemplifies the title of the book, 'Don't Let the Football Get in the Way of a Great Day Out'.

Some fans go to every single away game, others to as many as they can and some just a sprinkling. Each away game involves a major time (and monetary) commitment and not everyone can spare either, or regularly. I'm a 'go to four or five away games a season' guy. What are you?

One of my most memorable away games involved diarrhoea. Now this probably breaks every rule an author should follow and it can't be a sound plan when the reader sees any of your written words and goes, "Yuck!" However, it is an accurate representation of one of my favourite trips and we remember dates and events in funny ways and this is my way of recalling a great trip to Loftus Road in October 1989. Incidentally, my bad tummy has cleared up since then!

I booked a coach up on my team's Official Supporters Club that included a guided tour around the old Wembley, before driving onto my team's away game at Queens Park Rangers. It was a good price, something I had always wanted to do and we had a good team, so I took our 8 year old son Tristan with me. What could go wrong? Well, plenty as it turned out! I was really looking forward to the day and liked QPR's ground, as even then, it was old school and of course, relatively, it's even more so now. Unfortunately, when my rumbling tummy developed into multiple visits to the toilet during the night, I knew I was in trouble. I came to the flawed assumption that there was not much excess still to be ejected by my body, so I should be OK. I was wrong!

I made it up to Wembley, but then spent some time in a rather grubby public toilet in the Wembley car park. The tour was superb and we touched the bar where Geoff Hurst's shot bounced IN (not on the line and there was no VAR then) against West Germany in the 1966 World Cup Final. Then, we were on our way to see my team and for me, via that same public convenience.

As usual, QPR put the away fans behind the goal and my team's fans got top and bottom tiers. My team's support that day was excellent, although I found out that football grounds are not places to be stuck in, when your tummy is poorly. However, I didn't miss one goal (you must get your priorities right) and my team won 4-1, with a classy attacking display. My team's goal scorers that day say it all, with Rod Wallace getting two, Matt Le Tissier one and Alan Shearer one, so no wonder it was memorable. Not a bad forward line and all under 21 at the time. It was great fun between my retreats to the back of the stand and Tristan loved it and started his own lifelong love of football (but I did lose him to Chelsea).

I'm really pleased I didn't let my medical condition stop me experiencing this day and it did give me a great memory hook! Incidentally, diarrhoea is nearly as much a nightmare when you spellcheck it, as when you suffer it. You could say, its alternative spellings are loose!

John who sits behind me at my team's home games, goes to virtually every away game and is a great supporter of my team. Every club has these people who you see at every away game that you go to. You probably have these in your club and you may even be one yourself and if so, well done. Newcastle John told me that when attending his team's away games, as always Newcastle are well supported in numbers, but that it's a different atmosphere to home games, with a level of love for the team, several notches more intense. He says that if an away fan criticises the team, it's not unusual to be strongly rebuked themselves by a passionate Geordie (no doubt, often a bit overweight and naked from the waist up) to, "Get off the lad's back you!"

A more recent great away day for me was at Burnley in the Premier league and this just goes to prove again, memorable away days can often involve losses of bodily fluids, as well as matches.

The scene was set; my wife was out for a Christmas party and my team were away at Burnley and my friend Alan, who as you know by now, is a passionate West Ham season ticket holder, had told me that Burnley is a great place for an away trip. Therefore, what a good idea, so Glenn and I booked ourselves a couple of rooms for after the match, at a crazily cheap price in a little Pennine four-star hotel, 18 miles from Burnley.

Alan told me that Burnley were very welcoming to away fans and that Burnley Cricket Club was next door to Turf Moor and allowed away fans to park there and drink in the clubhouse. He had clearly had an enjoyable trip to the Cricket Club with West Ham, so it was a simple choice. He even added that on one early season visit there was a cricket match playing and he witnessed the odd spectacle of hundreds of West Ham United football fans cheering every wicket.

It all sounded very welcoming, so we purchased our Burnley tickets and did so with ease. It was a cold December weekend and in fact when we reached Burnley and the surrounding area, there was snow on the hills. However, the day was pleasant and sunny, plus our trip up was excellent, giving us plenty of time to experience Burnley Cricket Club. We were in good spirits after a full English at the Little Chef just south of the M40 and a 'trouble free' trip to the North. Unfortunately, this trend did not continue!

Burnley Cricket Club was exactly as Alan described it; easy to find, right by Turf Moor, cheap parking and with the old school Cricket Clubhouse on three levels ready to welcome away fans in three bars. We paid our fee and parked on the drive (this is relevant later) and we were welcomed into the clubhouse.

That day, my team took about 2,500 fans and many were enjoying the clubhouse hospitality and happily mixing with locals, although most in the building were wearing away team colours. We went to the bar on the second floor that had a balcony that overlooked the mothballed cricket pitch. We purchased some beers and a sandwich and settled down for some pre-match chatting and relaxation. You probably know that feeling yourself of anticipation, excitement and socialising before the match - it's priceless. We took our beers onto the balcony and enjoyed the surprisingly warm December sun on our faces and watched dozens of young away fans playing a friendly game of football on the cricket pitch with their home fans counterparts. It was idyllic and enhanced by the warming nature of the beer, so I felt I had to text Alan and thank him for his advice. I texted, "What a welcoming place for away fans - thanks mate!"

As I pressed 'Send', at that very moment, there was a loud noise coming from the ground floor at the front of the building, plus the sound of breaking glass and shouting. Something was going on. It didn't last too long, but clearly a disturbance had happened to shatter the calm of the Cricket Club. When we eventually left the building to make our way to the ground, which was next door, it was clear there had been a fight at the front door with broken glass everywhere.

The Burnley Cricket Club employee on the door said to us, "We never have trouble here, but some Burnley fans came in being idiots and some of your lot didn't like it. In all honesty, the Burnley fans got what they deserved, but don't let it stop you coming back next season, as this never happens here." He seemed genuinely upset that this had happened at HIS cricket club.

My team lost the game 1-0 and even managed to miss a penalty right in front of us, so at skin deep level it was a poor trip. As we disappointedly made our way back to the car up the drive of the Cricket Club, we could hear that unmistakable sound of 'football trouble.' That over-excited male yelling, interspersed with loud noises, that forms itself as a sort of mass rumble sound - it was like going back to the 1970s and I knew this background sound very well.

When we made it to the car, it was clear that trouble had occurred by my car and not only that, but in fact ON IT; then down the driveway and was now in full throttle outside the Cricket Clubhouse. The evidence was indisputable, as there was a lot of blood ON the bonnet of my white car and then a trail of red droplets that gave a tell-tale route to the clubhouse. You didn't need to be Hercule Poirot to work out what had happened and was in fact still happening!

We made our exit out of the drive rapidly as hordes of police cars and policemen descended upon the Cricket Club. I'm guessing that the very same Burnley troublemakers who were there earlier, but outnumbered heavily, came back with plenty of buddies, it certainly sounded like that. If you were a fan who was innocently involved and hurt that day, I am sympathetic. Of course, I have no idea what the true facts are, just what our friendly doorman told us.

However, once I cleaned the bonnet of blood, the dinner at the hotel that night was excellent and the setting magnificent and as usual,

Glenn and I analysed every aspect of why we lost, but this time beside a roaring log fire; like two male Charles Dicken's characters. We could only talk about two things; the penalty miss and the trouble. It was a very enjoyable trip and win or lose, but it's always fun to follow your team away. There is a certain bonhomie amongst away fans that you can't beat. My friends who support other teams, say exactly the same thing, some even recommend Burnley Cricket Club!

There is something about an away day at Burnley as friend and colleague Ipswich Stuart told me of his own memorable trip there on 16th August 2008. Apparently, it was the start of the season and Burnley celebrated this fact by arranging a number of sky divers (no VAR then) freefalling into the centre circle. All went well until the last Sky Diver was blown of course and ended up stuck hanging from the roof of the old stand. You might even remember this story yourself, as it was strongly featured on the news (incidentally, if you were the Sky Diver – apologies).

Stuart reflected to me that it was all very amusing and lots of fun was had by the away fans. However, despite Ipswich winning 3-0, the last laugh was on the football gods. As a result of the sky diving mishap, the match started 45 minutes late and Stuart and his friends missed their trains home and had to get an expensive taxi to Manchester Railway Station and then come home via two changes. On top of this, there was a fire at Wolverhampton Station and they didn't arrive home until early the next morning. What is it about away games at Burnley?

Now-a-days, fighting at football games is very unusual and if you keep yourself to yourself and don't go out of your way to illicit negative responses, you can generally wear your colours wherever you go (maybe not to your rival city) and be safe. Quite frankly this is how it should be, as all the other team's fans are doing is also passionately supporting their team.

Friend and business associate Alan of West Ham fame also told me of a highly enjoyable visit to Anfield in December 2013 when his team lost 4-1, but he loved every minute of the trip with his family. That's what away games are all about – the experience. Let's face it, unless you are a Top Six team, the statistical chance is you will lose more times than not when away from home!

There are a number of things I particularly love about away day jaunts and these include; the bonhomie amongst the fans (you don't get this so easily at home games), everyone sings, you can stand up, the anticipation, the trip and the inevitable full English breakfast, a few beers, randomly meeting some old acquaintances, stopping off on the way home for dinner or better still, staying over at a hotel, that underdog thing rather than expecting to win, which does take the pressure off and reduces expectations – well, in fact, just the experience!

Do you agree with this list and do you have any other special things that you love about away days?

Therefore, my Burnley away experience was a slight aberration and Burnley would have been one place I would not have expected trouble and certainly based upon what my friend Alan had told me about his West Ham visit there. This was how it was for us that day also, until a handful of people started it all, but isn't that how life is generally, the minority can ruin it for the majority?

A footnote to this story is that Alan has been back to Burnley FC twice since with his beloved West Ham and he told me that in the last trip, he was talking to the steward at Burnley Cricket Club. Alan asked him if they ever have trouble at the Cricket Club with away fans and his reply was, "Only when those Southampton lot come here!"

I suspect it was the same doorman who spoke to us!

Perspective is everything, isn't it?

It wasn't a quiet day for me in Burnley, far from it, but it was still fun and next time we can, we will go back to Burnley Cricket Club, without any fears, but this time, with a kitchen towel ready in the car!

Chapter 15

The Prawn Sandwich Affect

The profile of people attending football games in the modern era is very different to the 1960s and 1970s, well basically any era other than the modern Premier league era.

It was Roy Keane who typically outspokenly first opened the debate to describe the modern corporate box style attendees at games. The term 'Prawn Sandwich Affect' originated from a media comment by the Manchester United captain who felt certain sections of the Old Trafford crowd had not been vocal enough in their support and at times too quick to criticise minor mistakes, during their Champions League game against Dynamo Kiev in November 2000. He said, "Away from home our fans are fantastic, I'd call them the hardcore fans. But, at home they have a few drinks and probably the prawn sandwiches and they don't realise what's going on out on the pitch."

The term 'Prawn Sandwich Brigade' is often attributed to a direct Keane quote, but in fact the term originated in the print media in their reaction to Keane's comments. I think Roy was being a bit harsh with what he said, as only a small percentage of the crowd participate in prawn sandwiches, but the big picture message was relevant.

Incidentally, I have always found Manchester United's AWAY fans to be the best and most consistent and innovative singers, of all Premier League away fans. Do you agree?

The trend Roy Keane was looking to highlight was valid, if somewhat exaggerated. When I started watching football in the 1960s and 1970s the percentage of manual workers in the UK was 67%, whereas today that figure is around 45%. Inevitably, this social change reflects itself in the profile of crowds at football matches. Football was primarily a working class sport in the 1970s and as a result, priced accordingly. Now-a-days it's not!

In fact, the big changes have occurred in the last 20 years, well since the Premier League era really. When I first went with our son Tristan to watch his team Chelsea at Stamford Bridge, the Matthew Harding stand was a raucous place, full of die-hard Chelsea fans. When I went a few years later, I had Norwegian tourists one side and Japanese football tourists the other side. Now, I have nothing against foreign visitors, they and their money are warmly welcome, certainly as far as I am concerned. However, their presence is bound to negatively impact on the overall atmosphere and it does.

Of course, the average cost of seats has an impact and again at Chelsea on another day, our son Tristan took me into a wild and very intimidating pub near the ground, that was verging on crazy. Please note that we have gone from me 'taking him' to games to him 'taking me'! I got the impression that on match days this pub was a 'no go' venue for police and away fans alike. I also noticed that no-one in the pub left to watch the actual game, they stayed where they were and watched it on an illegal Russian TV channel and all got drunk and very angry with life!

It seems the cost of football now-a-days is stopping hard core fans actually attending games, although I suspect the police don't complain too much about that, judging by the behaviours in that pub pre-match!

Our son in law Jon of Norwich fame and our son Tristan, now added to by our youngest daughter's partner Wil and I, go abroad each year on a boys' trip to watch some exciting overseas game (more on this in Chapter 20) and in the last couple of years we went to watch Nice play PSG. It was a big game with a full house, but the tickets behind the goal were dirt cheap (less than £15 each).

The atmosphere was amazing (again more on this later), but was the lower price of tickets a factor positively impacting on the atmosphere? I suspect it was.

One thing that has improved over the years, is we now have many more women attending football matches, as well as children and this has to be good. We need families to go along to watch live matches and not just watch on TV or the internet. It's such a different experience live, isn't it?

One thing that has improved at games over the years, is the catering (not just prawn sandwiches) and I'm afraid Norwich Jon, this brings us on to 28th February 2005!

This was the day that celebrity chef and Norwich City director and supporter Delia Smith, grabbed a microphone at halftime during the match against Manchester City at Carrow Road. The game was 2-2 at half-time before Delia asked the fans, "Where are you" and implored them to support the home team.

She used the classic Norfolk call to action, "Let's be avin' you!" The suggestion has been made that she had enjoyed a little too much corporate hospitality red wine, but she subsequently categorically denies that she was tipsy. If she wasn't, I have to say she was impressively relaxed and great fun!

It really was hilarious and from my neutral point of view, it just made me love her even more. I say there is nothing wrong with a bit of unbridled passion!

I'm afraid Jon and many Norwich fans found the whole episode embarrassing, but I thought she was superbly funny and passionate. Unfortunately, it didn't work and Norwich went on to lose the game 3-2 with a last minute winner by Robbie Fowler and to make matters worse, Norwich were relegated that season (along with my team).

Am I the only one that finds Delia strangely alluring and attractive, in a school matronly kind of way; you have to love women (or men) who can cook?

Enough of this daydreaming about sexy mature celebrity chefs who love football, let's move on to politically incorrect, real men's food!

I refer of course to 'Pie and Mash', from the heart of the East End of

London. Let me first inform you that I have some East End heritage myself, with my grandmother being born and bred within the sound of the proverbial Bow Bells. This isn't strictly true, as Bow Bells are the bells of the church of St. Mary-le-Bow, Cheapside, London and this is actually west of my grandmother's real home, but why ruin a good tale and a nice phrase, with the truth?

My grandmother moved to Hampshire to avoid the bombings in the First World War, but never lost her strong Cockney accent or tough, matter of fact, "Give it eer', I'll do it for you", approach to life. Her East End roots were exemplified by her love of eels. Many years ago, when she was still alive, my brother worked at a manufacturing company that used river water in its processes and eels in the river were a pest. As a result, he would bring live eels home from work and give them to my grandmother. She kept them alive, swimming around in a bowl in her sink, until she was ready for a feast.

I remember one day visiting her when she was in her 80s and she said to me, "Are you hungry lad, I'm going to cook my lunch?" I said I wasn't and she then proceeded to pick an eel from the bowl, put its head against the wall, hammer a nail through its head (instantly and humanely killing it, I add) slicing a sharp knife down its length so the innards fell out, pulling the meat out in one roll, rinsing it and then throwing it into a waiting frying pan, all in 30 seconds flat. As a young teenager I was horrified, but she was having none of this and said to me, "That's what you call fresh!"

I understand from my cousin Theresa, who is much older than me (by 6 months) that I escaped that day, because she once got asked to nail the eel to the post!

I tell this story to highlight several things; how East Enders love eels, how matter of fact and tough was my grandmother and what a wimp I am!

My friend and business associate Alan sometimes kindly takes me to a West Ham home game and on occasions we have stopped at one of those Pie and Mash shops. He loves them. If you haven't experienced them, they are like Fish and Chip shops, but specialise in meat pies and mashed potato. So far, that's not too extreme, is it? However, the sting is literally in the tail, in the form of what they call, 'Liquor'!

Liquor is a sauce that is poured over the Pie and Mash and it's green in colour. It's non-alcoholic, despite its title and is made using the water kept from the preparation of stewed eels (that become Jellied Eels). The sauce traditionally has a green colour, from the parsley that's added. Basically, 'Liquor' looks like green gunge and to be frank, has the consistency like something that runs out of your nose when you have a heavy cold!

East Enders love it and if you ever go to visit, try it, although I suspect you will agree with my assessment of this East End delicacy.

Forget the catering though, whether you are sophisticated or hard core Cockney, if we want all these worldwide football stars to watch each week, I guess we have to accept it needs higher gate receipts at our clubs and the inevitable diminished hard core atmosphere. It seems that this is the price of change and there really is no going back.

In truth, previous footballing times really weren't perfect. Muddy, sandy, bogs of pitches, filthy toilets, dangerous cramming-in of fans, smoke-filled atmospheres, heavy duty footballs, anything goes refereeing and hooliganism – but very few prawn sandwiches!

In reality, not everything was better back then, but it has to be said; "I quite like prawn sandwiches, but definitely not Liquor!

Chapter 16

Memorably Great Teams

Great is a word that is used too loosely when referring to footballers and football teams. The dictionary defines 'great' as: "Considerably above average, substantial, pronounced, sizeable, appreciable, serious, exceptional, inordinate, extraordinary, special, prodigious, stupendous, tremendous, boundless."

This chapter covers great British teams of the last 55 years and I have attempted to ensure that the correct definition is rigidly applied, although inevitably the teams included are based upon my very personal assessment, so apologies if I missed any of your own favourites, or even your own team.

I start in 1967 and not with an English team, but a Scottish team and that is of course, Glasgow Celtic. I was 12 years old and on 25th May 1967, came in from kicking the ball around on the field with some mates, to watch, on a black and white TV, Celtic aim to be the first ever British team to win the European Cup.

It was a magical game in Lisbon Portugal, made better by the atmosphere generated by tens of thousands of Celtic fans. Inter Milan were a formidable, tough tackling, well organised outfit and yet Celtic hammered them. It was only 2-1, but Celtic had 42 shots to Inter's paltry 3 and had 10 corners to Milan's nil. These statistics say it all about the match. Their legendary manager Jock Stein said, "We did it playing football. Pure, beautiful, inventive football" and he was right. As a 12 year old this was a magical memory and just as with typical Home Countries' ways; English fans support Scotland when their team isn't playing themselves, but Scottish fans support whoever England is playing! This was how it was on 25th May 1967; a British team won the European Cup!

The next great team I remember from these shores was of course the first English team to win the European Cup and that was Manchester United in 1968. It was another evening game, but the bonus here was that the final was held at Wembley Stadium, which made the game virtually a home game for United. After the Munich Air crash tragedy and the Busby Babes era, there was immense emotional support for Manchester United from all across the country (possibly not Liverpool, but maybe even from there, back then).

After a great home cooked meal by my mum (probably Cottage Pie) and a quick kick around in the garden, the whole family sat down to watch the match between Manchester United and Benfica, who included the great Eusëbio. We still only had a black and white TV set, as colour TV sets didn't arrive until the early 1970s. Manchester United's team included Alex Stepney, Pat Crerand, Nobby Stiles, George Best and Bobby Charlton and was still managed by Matt Busby who was the manager at the time of the Munch Air Disaster, some 10 years earlier. Matt was on a mission to win the European Cup, that the air crash robbed his talented team of in 1958, when the crash happened after they had won the quarter final tie in Zagreb.

To get to the final back then you had to win four ties, as the only teams you played, were genuine league winners in their country. However, the semi-final against Real Madrid was an epic tie with Manchester United drawing the semi-final second leg 3-3 in Madrid.

In the final, Bobby Charlton scored first and Manchester United led 1-0 until Graca equalised with 11 minutes to go and heartache for the country, most of which were supporting United. A mention here for friend and associate John the Newcastle United fan who intensely dislikes people referring to Manchester United as 'United' as if there is only ONE 'United' whereas of course his beloved Newcastle United are one such team. I digress!

We need not have worried as in extra time, Manchester United (is that better John) scored three goals in five minutes from Best, Charlton and Kidd and the game was over and the second half of extra time was a celebratory procession. The classic key goal was George Best's magical dribble around the keeper, which has been much replayed ever since. This Manchester United team were a great team with a great manager and this night was their big night and we all celebrated in front of the TV screen with them.

Of course, above all else, Brazil 1970 was without doubt the greatest football team I ever watched play and they say all those amazing skills were learned by playing football on the beach. If you have ever tried playing football on a soft sandy beach, then you will know why they say that's the reason Pelé was so great!

All of the teams I cover in this chapter, other than Brazil and Glasgow Celtic have won the English top league, either the old First Division, or the Premier League and I have referred to games I watched myself. This has meant games often featuring my team, but rest assured and take comfort other teams' supporters, we inevitably lost, as these teams were great teams and my team tragically, were not!

One of these great teams however was more known for not winning any trophy, rather than winning. This was the great Leeds United team of 1971-72 season and surrounding era. Leeds did win the league in 1968-69 and 1973-74, but the team I refer to was the 1971-72 team. In fact, Leeds United came second in the First Division three seasons in a row; from 1969-70 to 1971-72 and this probably accounts for their fame for 'not winning'. It's wholly unfair of course and they were a great team. However, their game from this season against my team, was one of the most difficult losses to take as a fan. The result; Leeds United beat my team 7-0 on 4th March 1972 at Elland Road.

Leeds were an excellent team and at the time my team were not, but the problem was that this game was the featured game on BBC Match of the Day. Once Leeds were out of sight, they decided to take the mickey out of my team and did this very well. Johnny Giles and Billy Bremner were to be seen undertaking little flicks and keeping possession for several minutes with my team's players desperately trying to get in tackles. It was men against boys and very embarrassing. As you can imagine, the BBC played this repeatedly and rolled it out of the archives at intervals, for years and years.

Watching Leeds waltz around my team's defence at will, was a salutary lesson in humility.

However, they had to suffer their own lesson in humility when Derby County and their beach-like pitch pipped them to the league in 1971-72 and then worse still, Glasgow Celtic beat them in the previous season epic European Cup semi-final, with the second leg played at Hampden Park in front of an amazing crowd of 136,505. I remember that game well; Celtic and their crowd were unstoppable!

Nottingham Forest in the late 1970s were the best team in the league by a country mile and were managed by the unique Brian Clough. They won the First Division title in 1977-78 the season straight after promotion from the Second Division (they only finished third in the Second Division). Can you imagine that happening today? They came second in 1978-79 and won the European Cup two seasons on the trot; 1978-79 and 1979-90. They also won the League Cup in 1977-78 and 1978-79. It was the game against my team in the 1979 League Cup Final at Wembley that I remember the most. I have covered this in my most traumatic games, so I won't revisit the trauma yet again. Suffix to say, once Forest got their teeth into the game, there was no stopping them. They were a great team, rather than a team of great players.

Liverpool FC may or may not be your cup of tea (as they generally top the dislike league when other fans are surveyed), but it has to be said that today's fans pride in their club, is based upon a truly great era for Liverpool FC and their many great teams. Liverpool won the league in 1975-76, 1976-77, 1979-80, 1981-82, 1982-83, 1983-84, 1985-86 and 1989-90. They also won the European Cup in 1976-77, 1977-78, 1980-81, 1983-84, 2004-05 (sorry Liverpool fan Wil, nearly forgot this one) and now 2018-19, to date and at the time of writing. They did this with essentially, several different teams and in fact, different managers.

For a change, my memory of my team's game against this truly great Liverpool team was a happy one and this was in the 1983-84 season at home on 16th March 1984 when Danny Wallace scored one of my team's greatest goals. You must look it up on YouTube (I know you won't). Strangely, it was a Friday night game also, so I guess on TV as well, I'm not sure if the BBC had rights back then or not. Liverpool lost 2-0 and they didn't lose many that season, as they won the European Cup and the First Division title. It was my team's best-ever season, finishing second by only three points to this truly great Liverpool team. Happy memories!

A very similar regime and era followed for another great team, Manchester United (not United John) who between 1992-93 season and 2012-13 season won the league title 13 out of 21 seasons. Now that's domination over two decades. Again, they did it with several different teams, including the 'Class of 92' side, but importantly with one manager, the great Sir Alex Ferguson. I have picked two games I watched against Manchester United in this long period and both have become rather infamous across football fans of other clubs. In fact, both are connected by an inaccurate urban myth; I will explain.

Many fans have heard about the 'Grey Shirts' legend when Manchester United were being so badly beaten at the old Dell that at half-time they changed their shirts from the grey first half shirts, that apparently were the cause for their downfall, to blue shirts. United were a great, but aloof side and British people love it when the person at the top, slips up and onto their backside. Brings them down to earth, so to speak.

That's why the 'Grey Shirts' story became legendary. However, only part of the Grey Shirt urban myth is accurate. Yes, United did change grey shirts at half time after a battering in the first half, but this wasn't the legendary 6-3 loss to my team, but actually occurred on 13th April 1996 in the season 1995-96. Manchester United were losing 3-0 at half time, changed their grey shirts and ended-up losing 3-1, so maybe their beastly grey shirts were defective!

The game many people confuse with the Grey Shirt game, was the match on 26ᵗʰ October 1996 when my team beat Manchester United 6-3, including a stunning Matt Le Tissier dribble and chip over Peter Schmeichel. It was a great win against a great team, but it wasn't the Grey Shirt game, although they were both in 1996. You have to love Urban Myths, don't you?

As always, when you play against a Top Six team and they lose, it's never your team that's played well, it's always something else; but the colour of the kit was a new excuse.

Do you remember your team beating someone and the press just focused on how bad the opposition were? Galling, isn't it?

Mention must be made of the Arsenal Invincibles of season 2003-04 who went the whole season undefeated and also of Jose Mourinho's Chelsea, who won the title three out of six seasons from 2004-05 to 2009-10. Paul the Greek's Manchester City are the latest wonderful team, made-up of highly paid, but great players from around the world and managed by another superb manager, Pep Guardiola.

Do we sense a trend with these great teams and that is they all had great managers?

I think we do!

Chapter 17

Money, Money, Money in a Rich Man's World

This chapter title is a take on the famous Abba song released in 1976. It's chorus states;
"Money, money, money,
Must be funny,
In the rich man's world.
Money, money, money,
Always sunny,
In the rich man's world"

It goes on to say; "Ah ha, ah ha", but I won't continue any more, as that isn't the point of this chapter!

Of course, football now-a-days really is a rich man's world, although this is a rather sexist statement. What about rich women? Perhaps they have more sense than to purchase a football club in England! Incidentally, that ABBA song's chorus, is a bit sexist, isn't it? Hopefully this wasn't a factor in both marriages breaking down - I doubt it (just joking)!

You need to be unbelievably rich to own a Premier League club and as a minimum, you need to be a billionaire. Many people don't even know how many millions there are in a billion, it's so far from a normal person's world and arithmetical capabilities.

You have to be rich to buy the TV Rights, you have to be financially comfortable to afford purchasing match tickets and you even have to have some spare money to purchase Sky or BT packages to watch the games on TV. It really is a rich man's (or woman's) world now, at all levels.

Go to a Premier League game today with your son, or in my case, your grandson (my granddaughters aren't interested) and a ticket, burger and chips, programme plus travel, will cost around £150 to £200. You may not need to be a rich man, but you do need to have some spare cash.

It's indisputable that football has become a business and as a result, it's all about money. As a fan, I don't like it, but have to accept it, as I can't change it.

Let's reflect on who these 'Rich Men' really are and how much money, money, money do they really have. We may as well look at the Top Six and in order of controlling shareholders' size of estimated wealth (which is clearly a broad based estimate and not accurate), they are:

Manchester City - Monsour bin Zayed Al Nahygen ... Abu Dhabi ... £17 billion
Chelsea - Roman Abramovich ... Russia ... £10 billion
Arsenal - Stan Kroenke ... USA ... £6 billion
Tottenham Hotspur - Joe Lewis and Daniel Levy ... British ... £5 billion
Manchester United - Glazer Family ... USA ... £3.5 billion
Liverpool - Fenway Sports Group ... USA ... £2 billion

That's a lot of wealth and as the song goes, "It must be funny" and it certainly is that! Note; only one British billionaire owner, no women and three USA owners.

Of course, it's all about the TV rights and the rapidly developing Premier League brand around the world. Quite amazingly, in the year 2000 Manchester United's sales revenues were only around £150 million per annum. Today that figure is around £600 million. Of course, the club is now allegedly worth around over £2 billion.

These figures simply stretch your mind's perception of reality, don't they? Let's not forget the players either, who in modern times, live a life most of us can only dream about.

We occasionally hear stories of players' excesses, such as £500.000 weddings, or £1 million pound jewellery, or a quarter of a million pounds sports cars, but in reality, we can all just guess at what having these riches feels like.

This is their typical third home!

According to Sportingintelligence's Global Sports Salaries Survey in 2017, the average annual wage in England's top-flight were £2,642,508 or £50,817 per week. The £2.6m average for a Premier League player was more than double the equivalent figure in the German Bundesliga (£1.26m) and players in Spain's La Liga earned an average of £1.68m annually, while the figure for Italy's Serie A is £1.33m.

Listen to this though! In the season 2018-19, this Premier League average wages increased by 50% to be more like £3.5 million per annum. Manchester United's average player wage in the season 2018-19 was just under £7 million per annum.

Now let's get that in perspective. It's the average, so the highest earners we read about, earn figures like £20 million plus a year. Have you noticed how the media, to make it more palatable to us mere mortals, quote the wages in weekly terms? When was the last time you quoted your own salary by what you earn a week? Do they think we are simple – well apparently?

These are the wages of rich men, who have little or nothing in common with the fans who adore them (until they move on, of course), but we carry on going and we carry on paying the entrance fees, don't we; because we love football and we love our team?

On my worst football experience on Friday 25th October 2019 when losing 9-0 at home to Leicester City, my team had players on the field who simply appeared to give up like some schoolboy team and yet some were on wages of allegedly around £4 million per annum. Surely, at this level of pay, the least you can expect is hard work and trying their best?

Being poor is OK, but not trying; is a disgrace.

Money, money, money REALLY must be funny in a rich man's world!

Chapter 18

The Media – Love or Hate Them?

When I first discovered my passion for football, I was just a young boy and it was the 1960s. Football has changed so much since then, but so has the media.

My schoolboy room was full of scrapbooks, made-up of newspaper clippings of my team, that I had meticulously cut out of a newspaper, using scissors and then sellotaped into the page, with great attention to detail. Not so now-a-days and I suspect scrapbooks are a thing of the past. Some of our younger readers (but definitely not Paul the Greek) may not even know what a scrapbook looks like.

As a teenager or young adult, every Saturday evening I would walk a mile from our family home at exactly 6.30 p.m. to purchase for 10p, what we called 'The Pink'. It was the special Saturday evening sports edition of the local Daily Echo and its pages were pink – thus its nickname, 'the Pink'. It had the very first reaction and report on the local professional club's Saturday afternoon results and also the non-league results, which was the first chance you had to get these results. Of course, in those days, all games were on Saturday afternoon at 3.00 p.m. and newspapers still had a key role in society.

I'm almost certain that if you are old enough, wherever you grew up, these quaint local Saturday evening special papers were also part of the Saturday football tradition. Maybe your own was 'The Blue', 'The Canary Yellow' or equivalent! I love my memories of this cute Saturday evening tradition.

Some more newspaper memories from a previous era were my first family holidays abroad in the pre-internet days when the only way to get the latest football results was to go to a news stand in the country you were staying, the NEXT DAY and get your team's results. Telephone calls home were extortionately expensive and mobile phones hadn't been invented, so the next day's English newspapers were the ONLY answer.

Of course, it's the internet that made all these quaint traditions redundant. Today, we live in a world of Social Media, Twitter and ITKs (In the Knows) and every player transfer is signposted weeks ahead of clubs announcing their latest signing.

Not so in 1980, when my team produced pretty much the greatest transfer shock, EVER!

We may not have lived in the internet world then, but even so, newspaper journalists had their contacts, but this one slipped through their net. However, when my dad called me at work and said to me, "Wait for this, we have just signed Kevin Keegan!" I simply didn't believe him. Those of you as old as me, will remember what an incredible piece of news this was and what a coup?

I simply wouldn't believe my dad and it was only when my mum took the phone and told me, "It's true, really" that this wild piece of news started to sink in.

For those of you not around at the time, or not old enough, it really was like my team announcing they had signed Lionel Messi. Kevin Keegan was REIGNING European Footballer of the Year, having won it two years on the trot in 1979 and 1980, whilst playing for Hamburg in Germany. Think Brighton signing Ronaldo at his peak in 2016.

On 23rd July 1980 in the afternoon, my club called a press conference at the Potters Heron hotel near Romsey. My team's manager Lawrie McMenemy told the media that they would be able to meet, "Someone who was going to play a big part in my team's future."

To everyone's astonishment, alongside Lawrie McMenemy as he walked into the press room was current Ballon D'Or winner, Kevin Keegan.

It's important to note that at the time, Keegan was no player in his twilight years, he was at his peak and at age 29, he was a star of the England international side and had won numerous trophies with Liverpool and Hamburg. He had been expected to leave Hamburg, but to one of Europe's biggest clubs, such as Real Madrid, but instead he chose one of Europe's, let's just say – smaller clubs!

It really was that amazing and if you look at Ballon D'Or winners around this era, you have Johann Cruyff, Franz Beckenbauer, Karl-Heinz Rumenigge, Paolo Rossi and Michel Platinini. Keegan was that good and my club had signed him! It was the most exciting time and Kevin Keegan said in his autobiography that when he arrived at the airport for the press conference, nobody caught on and it was just assumed he was flying in to do a commercial for Faberge. His dramatic appearance at the press conference was greeted with total astonishment. You can add me to this list of people astonished AND excited!

In those days press conferences mattered!

Today, the media seem to peruse Social Media picking up on fans chit chat and rumours and printing it as news. Football agents spread stories about their players in the hope of creating a story that might become reality.

One of the aspects of the modern media I particularly dislike is the tendency for TV and talk radio stations to employ only ex-players of Top Six teams, which just emphasises the bias. I also dislike these same players openly displaying their bias and support. Surely, if they are journalists, they need to be independent?

When one of your team's players is sought after by a bigger club, the media starts all the rumours and false news and it becomes inevitable that once they get their claws into you, the rumour becomes reality.

From my personal point of view of the media, I used to love them and now I think I might hate them, you may have your own point of view. It's such a shame, because the likes of Kenneth Wolstenholme, David Coleman and Brian Moore were truly great journalists.

Not to worry, now we have the internet – heh ho!

Chapter 19

Keyboard Developments

I'm not against the internet or a dinosaur, grumpy old man and in fact, in my day job I'm CEO of a software company!

However, and this is a big BUT, I am not at all enamoured with the internet chat room land of trolls and keyboard warriors. All decorum, respect of others and common decency seems to go out the window on the internet.

This is the land of TLAs (three letter acronyms and sort cuts such as, omg. lol, I8u etc. etc. – help or should I say 'lp'? I suspect many of its protagonists are 14 years old and stuck in their bedrooms, never to leave the keyboard. Apologies if this insults you, I never intended this – lol (which I think means either means 'Lots of Love' or 'Laugh Out Loud' – or both)!

Since I started writing books that people purchase (honestly, they do) and are marketed on the internet and Social Media, I have attracted a few Trolls. How empty must your life be to spend endless hours abusing people you don't know, never met before and never will meet?

The problem is that keyboard warriors don't have any fear, as they know they won't have to meet-up with the recipient of their vitriol. As a result, they can be completely fearless and say what they want, although words on the internet in a public place (as these sites are), are subject to the laws of libel. Not everyone knows this fact.

Every professional football club in Britain now has at least one and often many, fans' forums. On these forums, you will find many well informed and articulate members, who share one passion, their love of their team. Of course, it is warm and comfortable to share space with others who share your passion. It's like an old school gentlemen's club, but with one big exception. No one vets the members on these forums!

We do have Administrators, but what can they do really? I'm a member of a couple and as far as I can see, every post tends to finish in abuse and threats. They can't seem to agree on anything. I do post occasionally, but always regret it.

On one such occasion, I posted for the first match of the season some interesting facts about my team's first games of the seasons over the last 10 years. To which some hyper-intelligent member replied, "So what you twat!"

Would they do that to my face? I doubt it and that's the problem with keyboard warriors.

However, these forums are strangely addictive, aren't they? I pride myself on being a reasonably intelligent and well-rounded individual with a broad based interest in many things. Despite this, I do sometimes find myself apparently addictively logging in to my favourite site. I have to limit myself to one visit a day when I realise,

I'm slipping down the compulsive path again. Needless-to-say, Marion my wife, is quick to point this out to me!

When Championship Manager was originally released, I undisputedly became addicted and would wave Marion off to bed at 11.00 p.m. saying, "I will be up soon", only to stay another two hours trying to win the Champions League with Burnley FC. which was my selected team. Does this sound at all familiar? I took Burnley (then a League Two team) through three promotions until eventually I won the double and the next year the Champions League. Isn't it a sad inditement of thus light addiction that I still remember this so called 'achievement' all these years later?

If only I knew then, how my real Burnley experiences would turn out with blood on my car bonnet!

Boy, was that game addictive! What was your Championship Manager team, or do you still play the game?

Today, we have the FIFA games and be honest, are you ever so slightly addicted now? Oh dear!

Some current players foolishly participate in Twitter and are then surprised when uproar erupts over what they write impulsively. When you are paid millions of pounds a year to play, it is probably wise to just keep your head down and play football and that's especially true when you have little in common with the people reading your Tweets!

After a match when a player is tired and emotional, it's probably not a good time to sound off online, but that's just me being sensible. I know some clubs now have strict policies on this for players and this makes perfect sense to me.

Still, if the president of the most powerful country in the world does it, why not a Premier League star?

Oh, how I miss the beautiful simplicity of Teletext! On match days this was the only reliable way to follow your team's scores if you weren't at the match and not able to listen to a radio commentary. Do you remember staring at the TV screen as Teletext rolled over 7 or 8 pages until eventually it made it to your team's score? Joy of joys when you scored and agony when they did! Do you remember standing outside Radio Rentals shop windows watching the rolling Teletext scores with about half a dozen others? Now that was technology!

You can't fight progress and the internet has smashed to memory both Radio Rentals and Teletext, but we still remember them fondly, don't we?

Of course, the reality is that keyboard participation or even Teletext staring, is a million miles away from the sheer unadulterated passion of a live game.

"Omg; how did I say this?"

Chapter 20

European Sorties

Of course, not all football is played in the green and pleasant land that is Britain. Those techy Europeans love their football as well!

As covered in Chapter 15, once a year, Tristan our son, Jon our son in law, myself and now youngest daughter's partner Wil, aim to go abroad to watch a big game over a lad's long weekend. It's become a bit of a tradition and is my regular birthday and Christmas present. It's a classic boy's weekend away, with football as it's raison d'être, but far from its only benefits. As you know, I believe it's important not to let the football get in the way, of a good weekend away!

It all started with Real Madrid at the Santiago Bernabéu Stadium where we actually saw 'The Galactica's' including David Beckham, Michael Owen, Figo and Zidane playing on the same pitch. What an experience, but Real Madrid didn't even score with those players and lost 1-0 to Celta Vigo, so clearly nothing is predictable and everyone is human.

We went on to experience many great trips including AC Milan at the San Siro, which was two thirds empty (that was weird) and then Ajax versus Feyenoord. Now this really is a fierce and bitter rivalry and such is the aggression between these two, that away fans were banned from these games. We stayed at a hotel close to the ground and in all my years of watching football, I have never seen such outwardly aggressive hard-core and obvious heavy drinking at match.

Big Dutch guys were walking around in groups with a litre bottle of scotch for themselves, a three litre coke bottle and just making up their own massive scotch and cokes. They were all very drunk (understandably), but also angry and looking for someone to focus this anger on; which was difficult, because there were NO Feyenoord fans there!

We were very concerned that a group of Chelsea, Norwich and Southampton fans might just do – so we stayed drinking in the hotel bar (which wasn't quiet either).

It was utterly crazy outside the ground with heavy, heavy drinking, wild excitement and a constant bang of firecrackers and red flares. It was immensely hostile and unlike anything I have ever experienced. The police clearly let the fans express all this outside the ground, because once inside, the police were in total control and everything settled down. In fact, despite the nature of the match, the atmosphere was no better than a normal Premier League atmosphere. The comparison between outside and inside was huge and quite strange to experience.

We had organised and purchased Basle versus Zurich tickets for February, which is again a big rivalry. However, believe it or not, snow stopped us making this game and not, as you would expect, snow in Switzerland in February, but a 'white out' in England! Who would have believed it? However, we had the last laugh, as the game went ahead (without us there) but was then called-off because of floodlight failure.

Nice at home to PSG one May was an altogether wonderful experience. Firstly, the weather was superb and beautifully sunny and warm. We stayed in Nice near the train station and spent one idyllic day catching the train to Monaco and eating Pizza and drinking beer on a bar on the beach. It was a couple of weeks before the Monaco (or Monte Carlo, as I prefer) Grand Prix, so all the spectator stands were up, as were the barriers and we were able to experience the presence of this legendary motor race, including the hotel swimming pool and tunnel. It was a magical and fun day before the football on Day Two.

Nice at home to the biggest team in France involved a superb atmosphere. Other than the taxi driver dropping us right in the middle of a very scary high-rise estate near the ground, with groups of dodgy looking Mafia-style men hanging around, drinking directly out of red wine bottles and casually carving wood (I think the taxi driver did this deliberately), all went well. They didn't sell any real food in the ground itself, but once inside, the whole experience was one to remember.

We had tickets right in the middle top tier of the Nice Ultras and it was an invigorating experience. It wasn't at all aggressive, just loud and crazy. All around us Nice fans were wildly excited. When the teams came out, huge colourful flares exploded around us and we all looked at each other with that look that said, "What have we done, coming here?" However, our initial fears were unfounded as everyone was well behaved, but extremely loud and excitable.

One particular guy was there on his own and just in front of us and he jumped up and down and sang every single minute from half an hour before kick-off to game end. He never stopped and I don't exaggerate. Two lovely looking French girls, no more than 20 years old (I know, but really, I'm not a dirty old man) did exactly the same thing, but also added some wonderfully rhythmic dancing to their jigs and songs. The whole ground sang the songs, waved flags and supported their beloved Nice team – and it worked!

Nice won 3-1 and on the way back to the hotel on a bus crammed full, with flag waving, singing fans it was an ebullient party to remember.

Everyone raves about the Premier League atmosphere at grounds, but this was in a different league. We all agreed, it was the best atmosphere at a match any of us had experienced and that we should be humbler back home and less arrogant about our football and fans.

Paul the Greek says the same about a game in Salonika in a crowd of only 13,000. Germany is our next target and especially the renowned Borussia Dortmund's Signal Iduna Park, with a capacity of 81,365.

When my team made it into Europe again in the 2015-16 season and were drawn against Vitesse Arnhem, I was determined to make it over there and break my own overseas European virginity. Friend, colleague and co-mad supporter Glenn and I booked our flights and hotel before the ticket details were out and as a result, we had great flights and a wonderfully whacky boutique hotel within walking distance of Arnhem town centre. All was set for another of those memorable away trips that stays in the memory forever. We purchased four tickets from Arnhem in the home end to be safe and then we did get our own club's two tickets, which with six tickets purchased, showed that we intended to get to the game! The trip to Arnhem was in August and they were a wonderfully balmy warm few days. We booked two nights at the hotel and so could do 'a reckie' of the town on day one. First thing to say was that all the Dutch people were so friendly and we were made to feel very welcome, with the centre of town set-up as a form of Away Team Party Central with red and white draping's, screens and banners. Strictly speaking, as time would tell, not ALL the Dutch people turned out to be friendly!

My team's fans started coming into town in a sprinkling on the first night and as Day Two progressed, more arrived. We walked down to the party area around 10.30 a.m. and the fun started. It was all very friendly with Dutch fans and away fans mingling and sharing rounds of beers. The sun was beaming down, England thrashed Australia at cricket that day and it was like being on holiday. By mid to late afternoon, Glenn and I decided we had drunk enough beer and got enough sun - we are sensible like that!

We walked back to our hotel rooms, had a cold shower, chilled-out and were ready to get an early taxi to the ground.

I then received a text from my worried son in law Jon back home in England and it read, "Are you OK, we are worried about you?" Now my family do love me, but this level of concern was unusual. I replied, "Yes I'm great, having a brilliant time, why do you ask?" He told me that it was everywhere in the news and internet that all hell had let loose in Arnhem with fighting between Dutch fans and English fans. Glenn and I were amazed at this news, as when we left all was warm and friendly in the square.

There had been a mini riot and we missed it!

It may have been Feyenoord fans or simply a small group of 100 Vitesse Ultras, but it ruined a great and friendly party.

This wonderful trip was rounded off with the memory of sitting outside the bar of our hotel with Glenn, in the warm evening air, sipping cold beers and briefly chatting to the local radio commentator and one of my team's ex-managers. What nice fellas they were and on top of that, my team were through to the next round!

One of my great heroes from the 1990s was my team's home grown, give it everything, left back Francis Benali. Franny is a great example of how a whole career of unmitigated dedication and effort to basically one club, his hometown club, sets a player aside as a true club legend. How does Franny feel when he sees the modern day players and pantomime legends, who kiss their badge when they score and then they are off as soon as a better offer is on the table from a Big Six team?

Perhaps this is the type of cupboard love, we could all do without; but Franny's style of dedication, yes please, we can't get enough!

Since he retired, Franny has raised over a million pounds for charity with his marathon runs, cycling and challenges and so typical of the man. Original Benali shirts are now collectors' items. My friend and co-supporter Glenn avidly supported the whole 'Benali on Tour' stickers fun. The idea is simple. Fans take sticky back Francis Benali cards wherever they go in the world and then photograph the sticker in a prominent position, in for instance, a bar in Cambodia. Your team's fans may do something similar.

It's an amusing homage to a club legend and in my scouting trip in April 2016 to watch AC Milan, I had the chance to put a 'Benali on Tour' sticker in the San Siro – and I took it. Does your club have its own unsung, genuine hero, loved by your fans, but generally not so well known by football generally?

When my team actually played inter Milan at the San Siro in October 2016, as a lifelong fan this was another once in a lifetime experience, shared with 8,000 to 9,000 other fans. If you have been on one of these European adventures with your team, you will know how exciting the whole thing can be. As soon as you arrive at the airport, your fans are everywhere and this just continues throughout the trip.

On the day of the match, the local square is full of your fans and Social Media tells you the 'in' place to be and where your fans are gathered. There is a real bonhomie about this whole experience, isn't there – unless of course, it overflows into violence and riots, which it occasionally does?

In Milan that day, the place to be were the bars by the canal. A quick train ride took us there and we had a wonderfully relaxing, fun and classic Italian long lunch of pizza and red wine, shared with a lovely couple we met from Dorset. We could watch and hear the madness of the bars but sit in our little sophisticated cocoon - lovely!

The bars ran out of booze, which judging by the state of some of the young lads, was no bad thing. Another quick train trip to the ground and we were at the San Siro after a breath taking 100-foot slog to our designated terraces behind the goal, my memory is the tannoy was so loud and blasted out Euro Pop Disco muzac, which meant no pre-game atmosphere was possible.

However, for me just going to the San Siro, playing the legendary Inter Milan and seeing all those away fans in Italy, was worth it all.

Friend and colleague Stuart's team Ipswich Town were themselves at the San Siro stadium on 6th December 2001. Ipswich led the first leg 1-0 but were overpowered away to Inter Milan 4-1. However, as always this wasn't what it was all about for Stuart. There were 7,000

Ipswich fans there in a crowd of 25,358 and he told me that he just loved seeing so many fellow fans in one place, so far from home. They did the canals, walked around the Cathedral Square and just had fun meeting people they hadn't seen since their schooldays.

It sounds so similar to my own San Siro experience (we both lost, of course) and really it just goes to prove, yet again, that you mustn't let the football get in the way of a great few days in Milan.

Our son Tristan experienced something similar when he went to watch Chelsea at the Camp Nou facing the legendary Barcelona on 31st October 2006 in front of 98,000 fans. Tristan took his wife to this game, as they didn't have children yet back then. Oh, "How lovely", I hear you think. When you hear the full story, you may not think this anymore!

When at work in his lunch break, Tristan thought it would be a good idea to go to Barcelona to watch this match and Thomas Cook were working with Chelsea to send fans on packaged trips of return flight and match tickets. So far, so good, so he impulsively booked two packages there and then.

This was no romantic city short break, wandering around the beautiful city hand in hand and enjoying a glass of Sangria in the sun. Oh no, the flight took off from Gatwick at 6.00 a.m. and landed back the next morning at 3.00 a.m. They lived in Bristol at the time, which was a 3 hour car ride to Gatwick. Work out the logistics yourself.

When Tristan got home from work, he told me that he asked his wife Heather, "Do you fancy going to Barcelona?" She says, "Yes, that's sounds great" and no doubt was imagining strolling around the squares in the sun in a leisurely three day break.

Then, he told her she was going next Wednesday and gave her the schedule!

She was understandably livid, as he had not consulted her before booking. Tristan reflected to me that this was the most trouble he has ever been in with her, although she has since forgiven him, because strangely she did enjoy the experience.

Apparently, she now says it was one of those things in life that she wouldn't have missed for the world but would never ever again want to repeat it!

It was the classic situation of it's easier to ask for forgiveness than it is for permission!

Tristan told me that needless to say, the trip was hectic and loud. Chelsea fans took over the row of café bars leading to the ground, which is classic piece of English fans on tour abroad tactics. Chelsea took 5,000 fans, but as usual with Barcelona, the away fans are put in the very top tier in a caged enclosure and with no roof, you have no hope of hearing the away fans on TV – just like they planned!

The game kicked-off as they do in Spain at 10.00 p.m. and finished 2-2 with Drogba scoring the equaliser three minutes into injury time. Tristan told me that the Spanish Riot Police seemed to try very hard to start something, so they could use those big batons, by banning the Chelsea fans from weeing in the toilets, but everyone stayed safe and well, despite their efforts.

Tristan told me that they were kept in for one full hour after the match and after a coach trip to the airport, flight home and drive back to Bristol, they arrived home at 6.30 a.m. exactly one hour before he had to leave for work!

Paul of Manchester City fame remembers how he was listening on the radio as a child in 1978 to their game at Bayern Munich. He vowed to get to a City game as soon as he was old enough. Unfortunately, he had to wait for 30 years before he could fulfil this goal!

He has since made up for it, with a stream of overseas trips following City, with his favourite being Bayern Munich away (it was in the stars) during the October Beer Festival. Paul reports he was so 'relaxed' at the game which they lost 2-0, he slept (along with most City fans) throughout the game in a post-alcoholic haze. Literally, don't let the football get in the way of a good two days out!

It occurs to me that the San Siro has played a significant part in my and others' overseas football experiences and that I have been to the home of AC Milan and Inter Milan one more time than I have visited Banks Stadium, Walsall. Interesting, but not unexpected!

I preferred the Banks Stadium, but just like Heather, I wouldn't have missed the trip for the world.

Chapter 21

Don't Let the Football
Get in the Way

We all love football and are passionate about our clubs and that's what pulls us together with common experiences and similar emotional highs and traumas.

However, this very same passion can cause friction that can occasionally develop into havoc. Unfortunately, football support can very easily evolve into a form of tribalism that is quite frankly, not at all attractive. Don't we all need to celebrate each other's passion and always keep things in perspective. It really isn't life or death, although sometimes it can feel this way!

This intense passion for our teams can create pleasure, excitement and much fun and experiences. The flip side, as we all know, is that this deep passion can and does cause much pain, sometimes deep despair and occasionally, numbing disappointment.

Why do we do it then?

As I trudged back to my car on 25th October 2019, rain driving into my face, puddles over my shoes and dismayed having lost 9-0 at home that's exactly what I why said to myself!

One answer might be the hope of future highs, but so is the fact that once you fall in love, that's it, you are hooked. Clubs of different fans, experience different types of football feelings and if you are a Manchester City fan, no doubt you are 'frustrated and angry' when your team only finishes second in the league and wins ONLY one cup in a season. Fans of Newcastle United, Crystal Palace, Brighton, Burnley, Wolves and my team, to name just a few, are generally just happy when we stay up and watch a few exciting games. Not too much to ask, is it?

I suspect that promotion from League Two by finishing second, is just as exciting for fans of the club promoted, as winning the league with Manchester City. It's all a matter of perception and football at grass roots level is just as relevant as the great riches of the Premier League.

If you can bear it, try listening to those football phone-ins, especially post-match and there seem only two emotions; either wildly unrealistic happiness and expectations, "We are going to get in the Top Four" (the classic delusions of grandeur) or deeply frustrated and depressed to the point of suicidal. It's only a game, life is so much more important! There seems to be no 'in between'! It's entertaining to hear, but ONLY, if it's not your team, but not in the least bit pragmatic or realistic.

Of course, that's the point, football isn't meant to be pragmatic. It's all about emotions and passion and not logical at all. I believe this is best summed up by Alan of West Ham United's fame and his visit to old Trafford on the last game of the season on Sunday 13th May 2007.

West Ham needed to win to stay up and basically fellow relegation candidates, Sheffield United, not to win as well. Carlos Tevez scored for West Ham after 45 minutes and Alan was joyous.

Alan told me he spent the WHOLE of the second half looking at the big clock in the corner and hardly saw any of the game. Manchester

United had 25 shots (few of which Alan saw) but didn't score and West Ham stayed up.

We can all have empathy (other than Sheffield United fans) with Alan and his second half endurance and torture and doesn't that just about sum up what it's like to be a passionate football fan?

This is my problem when I read people on Social Media or hear them on phone-ins and that is fans talking about their clubs like they are playing Championship Manager or FIFA 2019. "We need to sell him for £25 million and then buy a centre half at £30 million and a midfielder at £50 million etc. etc." It's more like Monopoly, than a real passionate football supporting life. Unfortunately, this is the result of all the riches of the Premier League. When we spoke together as fans 30 or so years ago, we simply didn't talk about money. Now-a-days, money is never far away from fans conversations.

I find this sad, as football is about passion, loyalty, emotional highs and lows, experiences like travel, socialising, drinking and eating, a feeling of belonging and quite often, a sense of familiarity and routine. The same seat and rituals going to games ever couple of weeks.

It's the passion that we share, whoever we support and I hope that listening to some other fan's passionate experiences and reflecting on your first game, some old school hooliganism that were played in tin shacks, has helped connect with your own passions.

Then, of course there was the magic of the cup, those bitter rivalries, the amazing Kenneth Wolstenholme and all those England hurting experiences, which I'm afraid, haven't stopped yet!

We looked back at the blood and thunder of the 1970s, programmes and stickers and those rare geniuses and classic entertainers. We asked, "Is Your Club a BIG Club?" and whatever your answer we all suffer those gut wrenching moments and enjoy those away day jaunts. We reflected upon some great teams of the last 55 years, prawn sandwiches (we were hungry) and how money, money, money can get stuck in your gullet, in a non-rich man's world.

We didn't forget technology, the media and keyboard warriors and of course reflected on our own more successful Brexit, in the form of European Sorties!

After all this, there can be no other conclusion than that football is a great game, our passion is there to be celebrated and cherished. Above all else, we must never let the football get in the way of a great day out.

Enjoy many more great days out!

Other Books by the Author
www.richardwaltersauthor.co.uk

Aren't We a Funny Lot?

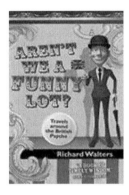

Brexit, Football hooligans, Friday-night binge drinking, NHS waiting lists, corrupt politicians – oh and the climate. There are seemingly endless things that make us despair of life in modern Britain. But in Aren't We a Funny Lot? Richard takes an altogether different, more cheerful tact.

From spotted dick to old school seaside holidays, to country pubs and the national obsession with tea, he reminds us what it is that makes Britain 'great'. In a series of chapters covering such diverse topics as sleep, sex and sunshine (or the lack of all three), he highlights the weird and wonderful idiosyncrasies that make us British what it is – sometimes just plain crazy!

Witty, insightful and razor-sharp, *Aren't We a Funny Lot?* will have you laughing out loud and it's possible 'crazy and whacky' might just be what we need in today's worryingly extremist modern world.

Aren't You Listening to Me?

With tongue in cheek, Richard and Marion Walters explore twenty of the most sweeping generalisations about men and provide some surprising facts about the battle of the sexes.

Even those unlikely bedfellows of men hating feminists and sexist men, can chuckle along with the rest of us, knowing that the female equivalent *Aren't You Ready Yet?* is there to balance things up!

This is a light, humorous dip-in book that you will be quoting to your friends, male and female and it might just challenge some of your own pre-conceptions about men (well maybe).

Aren't You Ready Yet?

Men and women are different and if you are a man it's important to better understand the fairer sex (yes, it's that word already) and if you are a woman, it's important to fight back against the lazy thinking surrounding your gender.

With tongue in cheek, Richard and Marion Walters explore twenty of the most sweeping generalisations about women and provide some surprising facts about the battle of the sexes. Even those unlikely bedfellows of men hating feminists and sexist men can chuckle along with the rest of us, knowing that the male equivalent *Aren't You Listening to Me?* isn't far away!

This is a light, humorous dip-in book that you will be quoting to your friends, male and female and it might just challenge some of your own preconceptions (well maybe).

Being an Entrepreneur

People who go into business and start or acquire their own businesses are a breed apart. We call these people entrepreneurs and small and medium sized businesses are the lifeblood of our society, creating wealth, moving products and services and employing the majority of the working population.

Business owners who become their own bosses have decided to; control their own destiny, take risks in exchange for potential rewards, be self-sufficient and back their own judgement. Entrepreneurs deserve to succeed because they take the risks and give absolutely everything to their businesses.

This book reflects upon the key aspects of being a successful, unique and passionate entrepreneur, which you will find affirming, enlightening and inspiring. Success in business and in life generally, requires belief, vision and action and it's always worth remembering that success really is a process, not a one-off event, especially for entrepreneurs.

Enjoy being inspired to achieve your goals, one step at a time.

97 Ways to Inspire You to Greater Business Success

Business owners tend to have passion and drive in abundance. Success is an emotive concept so it's important to find your success definition and then passionately go for it!

This book draws on Richard's experiences as a serial entrepreneur and provides 97 simple, but enlightening ideas for busy business owners over six chapters.

It's a dip-in book, so have fun and take what you want and feel is relevant to you.

Delivering Advisory Services

Accountants know they now need to develop structured advisory serves, but the big question is, "How do I do this when you are still busy?" There are many misconceptions and myths surrounding these advisory services and the book aims to fully explain truly client centric advisory services and how to easily develop fully structured and sustainable services that future proof accountancy firms.

It is an essential guide from start to finish for accountants and consultants interested in extending or developing advisory services to their clients and prospects.

Utilising his 25 years of experience as one of the original protagonists and leading experts on strategic advisory services for owner manged businesses, Richard takes you through how to easily get started in providing truly client centric, structured and lucrative services.

"The first 90 minutes are the most important."

The late, great
Sir Bobby Robson

"In football, everything is complicated by the presence of the opposite team."

Jean-Paul Sartre

Printed by Amazon Italia Logistica S.r.l.
Torrazza Piemonte (TO), Italy

10893732R00098